BETTING BASEBALL
2010

In his book "The Seven Habits of Highly Successful People", Steven Covey tells the story of a man cutting down a tree in the woods. "What are you doing?" he is asked.

"Can't you see?", the woodcutter impatiently replies. "I'm sawing down this tree."

"You look exhausted. How long have you been at it?"

"Over five hours," he answers, "and I'm beat. This is hard work."

"Well, why don't you take a break and go sharpen that saw?" you inquire. "I'm sure it will go a lot faster."

"I don't have time to sharpen the saw," the man says emphatically. "I'm too busy sawing!"

Betting Baseball 2010 is designed to "sharpen the saw" for baseball bettors. Just as reading a history book doesn't make one a top-notch historian, reading this book won't make a bettor a top-notch baseball handicapper. It will, however, provide you with the tools to put you on the way. A bettor should study this book, follow what he likes, reject what he doesn't, and refine whatever he needs. After all, it is his money on the line.

PeepsPlace.com is a sports forum that will have in-season updates and possible corrections to Betting Baseball 2010. Updates and revisions for this book were written by Hank Myers. Questions and comments for Mr. Myers may be sent to BettingBaseball2010@gmail.com. Earlier versions of Betting Baseball, and the bulk of this current work, was written by Michael Murray.

TABLE OF CONTENTS

MAXIMIZING PROFITS WITH SPORTSOPTIONS

This is NOT a paid advertisement. I asked Sportsoptions for a breakdown of their service because it is simply the best lines service available for a baseball bettor. The injury reports, real-time odds, and other tools give the bettor a huge edge when it comes to wagering. At the very least, take SO up on their free seven-day offer. I doubt you will be disappointed.
MM

For many players MLB season is the prime money making season. The number of games, lower juice and betting variety give even smaller players a great opportunity to build their bankroll. However, diving into the baseball season without the right tools can sink a player, causing them to make uneducated plays and laying bad prices.

With the larger number of games and huge rosters, keeping track of the available information can be a daunting task. Odds, lineups, starting pitchers and weather are constantly changing and missing out on just a few pieces of key information can sink you. Luckily today's players have an affordable solution – SportsOptions.

The SportsOptions service gives players access to real-time odds from over 60 sports books worldwide, the fastest lineups and breaking injuries, stadium weather updates, fast and accurate score updates, game matchups and team and player stats. So whether you are a stats-based handicapper, a strict value player or an arbitrager, you will get the information you need to play smarter.

So how can SportsOptions help you? Here are just a few examples:

- Real-time odds from over 60 sports books – One thing that all professional players agree on is that getting the best odds on all of your plays is key to making money. If you are making plays on a regular basis, having multiple accounts is an absolute must and having instant access to the available odds at those accounts ensures that you always get the price you are looking for.
- Injuries and lineups – With so many handicappers using player based systems in MLB, having fast and accurate lineups and injuries is a must and no single source is faster or more accurate than SportsOptions.

Whether you increase your play or get off a game, having the injury information first will ensure that you maximize the value.

- In depth gaming matchups and stats – The internet is filled with stats sites, but finding stats relative to your handicapping can be challenging. SportsOptions stats are gaming specific, so you get everything you need in just a few clicks. For every MLB game you will get game matchups, team related stats, pitcher stats, fielding and batting stats, umpire reports and stadium weather reports.

You can try SportsOptions free for 7 days. Just visit www.SportsOptions.com/free to create your account. There is absolutely no obligation and no credit card is needed to get the free trial.

MONEY MANAGEMENT

"Managing money requires more skill than making it."
Motilal Oswal

Betting baseball is simple. Just pick the winner. There are no point spreads to beat, and the reduced juice seems to be a gift. It is never that easy, however. Baseball is the most exhausting sport to bet. From February to October, it is constantly in the news. The season doesn't start in April; it begins during spring training when the optimism of every team permeates the landscape. Bettors fall prey to the same optimism. They spend all March listening to the talking heads and other self-proclaimed baseball experts. They do plenty of due diligence, never thinking that much of what they hear and read is simply noise rather than news. They know the hot pitchers coming out of spring training, have read what "unnamed scouts" are saying, and collect tiny pieces of information from coaches, managers and reporters that foretell how successful a team will be in the upcoming season.

In theory this is all good. In practice, danger lurks. All teams have agendas. Some want to sell more tickets. Some want to bump up a player's trade value. Or sometimes a simple decision gets rethought. A player who won his job in 75 spring training at-bats against suspect competition will lose his job once his first slump hits. Misinformation is commonplace in baseball. A bettor can think he knows enough, and think he knows how a game will play out, but in the end, the uncertainties carry the day. I have listed below some key points to surviving and prospering during the baseball season. Above all, common sense should rule the day:

- Money management means minimal exposure of your bankroll.
- Spread the risk; betting five games at 2% of your bankroll is far less risky than one game at 10%.
- Bet no more than you can afford to lose.
- Don't chase your losses.
- Winning isn't everything; if you can't enjoy a great baseball game because you had money on the losing side, you probably are betting too much on the game.
- Don't bet parlays. While a sophisticated bettor can find an edge in many parlays, winning a parlay may harm your money management skills later in the season. Keep it as simple as possible.
- Ignore your hunches.
- Don't vary your wager size by more than 50%. If your average wager is 2% of bankroll, keep your maximum bet at 3%.

- Locks are a myth. If a number looks way off, chances are you overlooked something the bookmaker hasn't.
- Review both your winning and losing bets. While it is important to understand why you lose, it is equally important to understand why you won.
- Don't be stupid.
- Don't be greedy.
- Keep a cool head.
- Understand that you have no control over what happens in a game. Once you play it, forget it. If winning or losing is so important to you regardless of the amount wagered, don't watch the game.
- Don't let the thrill of victory or the agony of defeat affect your next play.
- You are never as good as you think you are when you are hot, nor as bad as you think you are when you are cold.
- Be satisfied with any profit.
- Concern yourself more with what happens in the game than the outcome. Teams that dominate a game will often lose; in the long run, it is better to be right and lose than be wrong and win.
- Make your own line, and understand how the bookmaker makes his.
- Keep in mind that you will lose 10 games in a row at some point in the season, particularly if you play a lot of underdogs.
- Never get tired of other people's opinions.
- Never put too much stock in other people's opinions.
- Keep in mind that the line is the sum total of the ignorance of the betting public. Never overestimate the general public's ability to pick winners.
- Without discipline, there is no profit in gambling.

Money management is a defensive tactic in betting. It keeps you alive to bet again. Every day a bettor is going to see lines that look too good to be true. Without a system of risk control, that bettor is going to have problems surviving the losing streaks that are inevitable in baseball.

Probability rules baseball. Who wins or loses is secondary. If a coin landing on heads pays +110, is there any doubt which side should be bet? The ultimate goal of each baseball bettor should be to find these coin toss situations with the odds in his favor. Success in this guarantees success in betting. Mike Caro calls these the absolute truths of probability:

- You must eventually lose if the odds are against you.
- You must eventually win if the odds are in your favor.

- If skill affects the odds in any way, then skillful players will eventually fare better than unskilled players.

Putting the odds in your favor involves having a good process when betting baseball. A bettor should have a solid understanding of mathematics, a deep intelligence of the game, the willingness to use statistics, understand the principles of probability, and develop a plan of action that will ensure survival when the inevitable losing streak hits. A winning bettor is aware that the frequency of winning is not important; the frequency multiplied by the payout is what matters. Michael Mausboussim, an investment banker for First Boston, describes an investment matrix that looks like this:

	GOOD OUTCOME	BAD OUTCOME
GOOD PROCESS	Deserved Success	Bad Luck
BAD PROCESS	Dumb Luck	Poetic Justice

In the long run, it is better to lose sharp than it is to win stupid. When you are making around 10 plays a day for nearly 200 days, it is how well you play the game that really matters. Dumb Luck may win out over a period of time, but Poetic Justice is always lurking behind the corner.

Money management should be kept simple. A bettor should set his base bankroll each season, adjusting once that bankroll increases or decreases 10%. If you like to bet a lot of games, keep the base unit low (1% range). If you only bet a few games a day, or consider gambling a hobby using only your disposable income, a higher percentage of your bankroll can be justified. The cost of busting out is simply waiting until a few paydays come around.

There are other, more sophisticated money management systems out there. The Kelly Criterion is one of the more popular ones. Kelly is a complicated, aggressive system designed to maximize profit. Wikipedia.com describes the formula below:

$$f^* = \frac{bp - q}{b},$$

Where

f^* is the fraction of the current bankroll to wager;
b is the odds received on the wager;
p is the probability of winning;
q is the probability of losing, which is $1 - p$.

As an example, if a gamble has a 40% chance of winning (p = 0.40, q = 0.60), but the gambler receives 2-to-1 odds on a winning bet (b = 2), then the gambler should bet 10% of the bankroll at each opportunity (f* = 0.10), in order to maximize the long-run growth rate of the bankroll.

The Kelly Criterion boils down to this: the bigger your edge, the bigger your bet. It is a high risk, high reward method designed to maximize profits for a sports bettor. Using Kelly, a bettor has a 50% chance of losing half his payroll at some point. He has a 30% chance of losing 30% of his payroll.

Most bettors who follow the Kelly Criterion use variations of the method. Half Kelly is a dialed down version of the formula that lowers the risk to bettors. A 55% handicapper using half Kelly will have his average wager at 2.8%. In baseball, with the daily grind and thousands of betting chances over the course of a season, that is too high for most. Unless you have the experience and knowledge to know your true edge, it is best to avoid using variations of the Kelly Criterion.

STATISTICS

A bettor is bombarded with a wide range of statistics in today's baseball game. Obscure statistics like Relief Efficiency Rate may have some informational bases to a bettor, but in the grand scheme of things this statistic has little bearing on how well a team will perform.

There are hundreds of these types of stats in the game today. The free access to data, and massive explosion in statistical interest since Michael Lewis's "Moneyball" was released five years ago, has resulted in a similarly explosion in new ways to measure players and teams. VORP (Value over Replacement Player) is working its way into the mainstream lexicon. Win Shares is becoming an answer to the question of a player's worth. Win Probability Added uses play by play data to measure how much credit each player deserves for his team's victories. The list goes on and on. Do we want to know how well Detroit has hit against lefties in the last ten games? Or how the Tigers have hit on grass fields this year? Or at night? In a dome? Against a finesse pitcher? Against a fly-ball pitcher? It is all out there, and it is all free.

This wealth of information is certainly an improvement from years past for the average bettor. But there is a great danger in getting bogged down in the minutia and forgetting the big picture. A statistic doesn't replace good judgment. It doesn't replace common sense. And it certainly doesn't replace sound money management.

There is a great desire among baseball bettors to find the one perfect statistic that will point the way to prosperity. It is time to give this dream up. There isn't one magic number out there. Some circumstances require a hammer. Some require a screwdriver. Betting at baseball (or any sport) requires flexibility and the understanding to know when the hammer is needed and when it isn't. Do we really care how bad a shortstop Derek Jeter is when Joba Chamberlain is on the mound? Not really. Chamberlain is a strikeout machine who isn't dependent on his shortstop making plays to be successful. That wasn't true when Chien Ming Wang was on the mound for New York. An extreme ground-ball pitcher, Wang was hurt by the fact that the gold-glove shortstop for the Yankees can't field ground balls up the middle.

To be of consequence to a bettor, a statistic must primarily be useful in determining who wins or loses a baseball game. Nothing else. Stolen bases are one of those interesting historical statistics that fans, players, scouts and announcers often use to judge the quality of a player, but it has little impact in predicting the outcome of a baseball game. If you have time to kill, it might be fun to see how the Chicago Cubs controlled the running game. But speed likely won't matter in the outcome of a baseball game.

Only in hindsight is speed important to a gambler. If Juan Pierre bunts for a single, steals second base, then scores on two ground balls to break a 9th inning tie, speed will have made a difference. It is a waste of time, however, to handicap based on that possibility.

There are three conditions by which a statistic must be judged:

- It must be easy to understand. With fifteen games on the board every day, a statistic loses its purpose if it can't be used quickly and coherently.
- It must measure something important to winning a baseball game. Speed doesn't do this, so a team's stolen base information is irrelevant
- It must accurately measure what it is trying to measure. A pitcher's record is one example; the pitcher's individual win-loss record is too heavily dependent on his team to have any basis in handicapping.

If a statistic doesn't meet these criteria, throw it out. You won't need it.

Torture numbers and they'll confess to anything.
Gregg Easterbrook

Do not put your faith in what statistics say until you have carefully considered what they do not say.
William W. Watt

The theory of probabilities is at bottom nothing but common sense reduced to calculus.
Laplace, *Théorie analytique des probabilités*, 1820

I abhor averages. I like the individual case. A man may have six meals one day and none the next, making an average of three meals per day, but that is not a good way to live.
Louis D. Brandeis

He uses statistics as a drunken man uses lampposts - for support rather than for illumination.
Andrew Lang

BASICS OF BETTING BASEBALL

The typical baseball line looks like this at a sports book:

	TEAM	PITCHER	RUN LN		MONEY LN	TOTAL	
951	Rockies	Redman	+1.5	-104	+196	OVER 7	-116
952	Brewers	Sabathia	-1.5	-106	-214	UNDER 7	+106

This line says:

- The top team, Colorado, is the visiting team.
- The bottom team, Milwaukee, is the home team.
- Mark Redman is starting for the Rockies.
- C.C. Sabathia is starting for the Brewers.
- The Rockies plus 1.5 runs is –1.04.
- Milwaukee minus 1.5 runs is –1.06.
- Colorado is a +196 underdog.
- The Brewers are a –214 favorite.
- Over 7 is a –116 favorite.
- Under 7 is a +106 underdog.

The line also gives a few more details. The sports book is using a dime line on the Total, meaning that there is a 10-cent difference between the dog and the favorite. They also use it on the Run Line. Most sports books use a 20-cent line when offering Run Lines and Totals; action on Totals is usually more sophisticated and the book tries to minimize its risk. The sports book listed above doesn't have this fear. On the money line above you see an 18-cent difference between the favorite and dogs. This sports book (Pinnaclesports.com) uses an 8-cent line on the money line that graduates upward as the price of the favorite increases. For example, two evenly matched teams might each have a –104 line to win the game outright. If one team (like the Brewers above) is a heavy favorite, then that 8-cent spread will be larger.

Most books use a dime line; this has been standard practice since a Las Vegas book decided to attract customers by lowering its juice. Other books were forced to discount their vig to meet this competition and baseball bettors have been spoiled ever since. Baseball doesn't generate much positive revenue for books, particularly compared to football. The dime line is a major reason.

One aspect a bettor needs to know is the concept of listing pitchers when making wagers. Sports books take the above bet not as Colorado vs. Milwaukee but as Redman vs. Sabathia. If either pitcher doesn't start the game, the bet is cancelled and wager refunded.

To avoid this, an 'action' bet can be requested by the bettor. Action means a bettor will keep his bet regardless of any pitching changes. The sports book will readjust the payout odds, but the bettor will still have his wager. For example, if Ramirez is replaced by John Smoltz, Atlanta may become a –150 favorite. The bettor who originally had Atlanta –106 now has Atlanta –150.

It is usually a mistake to request an 'action' wager. At times it can be done; I may use action when I will be unable to re-make my wager and am betting against a team more than against a starting pitcher. But a starting pitcher has too much of an impact on the game to risk money on this unknown factor. Action bets also mean you are stuck with a book's "readjustment". This eliminates the ability to line-shop for value.

A SPORTS BOOK'S HOLD PERCENTAGE

To see the effect of the dime line on a sports book one must be familiar with the theoretical hold percentage (THP). THP is what a book expects to make under perfect conditions per $100 bet. In sports using point spreads, the THP is 4.55% assuming the book uses the standard bet 11 to win 10. Baseball is a bit trickier; the THP changes depending on the odds. The formula for THP is:

Step 1		1 – (1 + Dog Price)
Step 2	Multiplied by	(1 + Favorite Price)
Step 3	Divided by	1 + Dog Price
Step 4	Multiplied by	Favorite Price
Step 5	Plus	1
Step 6	Plus	Favorite Price

The THP is also expressed as:

$$1 - (1+\text{Dog Price}) * (1+\text{Favorite Price}) \text{ divided by}$$
$$((1 + \text{Dog Price}) * \text{Favorite Price} + 1 + \text{Favorite Price})$$

Here is Pinnacle's THP using the Mets/Braves match up shown earlier:
THP=1 - (1+196) * (1+214) / ((1+196) * 214 + 1 + 214)

The THP=1.90%. If there is $10,000 wagered on this game perfectly split with no line movements necessary, Pinnacle will hold $190.

Heavy volume is needed to make baseball profitable to a sports book like Pinnacle. One sports book goes a bit further than even Pinnacle. 5 Dimes.com offers a five-cent line on overnight wagers. There is a $500 per game limit on bets to protect the book from sophisticated bettors, but lines like that give unprecedented value to the recreational gambler. Below is a table detailing the THP for a sports book with a nickel line:

5-CENT THP	DOG PRICE	FAV PRICE	BOOK EARN ON 30K
1.20%	+1.00	-1.05	$361
1.10%	+1.10	-1.15	$328
1.00%	+1.20	-1.25	$300
0.92%	+1.30	-1.35	$274
0.84%	+1.40	-1.45	$252
0.78%	+1.50	-1.55	$233

Pinnacle's 8-cent line THP is listed below: After –1.90, the line breaks into a dime line.

8-CENT THP	DOG PRICE	FAV PRICE	BOOK EARN ON 30K
1.89%	+1.00	-1.08	$566
1.72%	+1.10	-1.18	$515
1.57%	+1.20	-1.28	$470
1.44%	+1.30	-1.38	$432
1.33%	+1.40	-1.48	$397
1.23%	+1.50	-1.58	$367

The majority of books use the dime line; some keep the dime line until the favorite hits –1.95. The dime line THP is listed below.

10-CENT THP	DOG PRICE	FAV PRICE	BOOK EARN ON 30K
2.33%	+1.00	-1.10	$697
2.12%	+1.10	-1.20	$635
1.94%	+1.20	-1.30	$581
1.78%	+1.30	-1.40	$533
1.64%	+1.40	-1.50	$491
1.52%	+1.50	-1.60	$454

A small minority of sports books still uses the 20-cent line. The THP may be up, but the handle typically is much lower. TheGreek.com is the best-known book that still uses the 20-cent line; their reputation is such that they don't need the reduced line to attract players. Other books simply would rather not take a whole lot of action on baseball.

20-CENT THP	DOG PRICE	FAV PRICE	BOOK EARN ON 30K
4.35%	+1.00	-1.20	$1304
3.98%	+1.10	-1.30	$1192
3.65%	+1.20	-1.40	$1094
3.36%	+1.30	-1.50	$1008
3.11%	+1.40	-1.60	$931
2.88%	+1.50	-1.70	$863

PHP Percentage

Odds on the games will move during the day. Sports books typically don't want to be too lopsided on one side and will adjust the line in order to balance out the action. So what moves the line?

One reason for the line move might be self-preservation for a book. If other sports books are moving the line one way, the sports book might move the line on "air" and follow suit without taking bets that would move the number by themselves. Books want even action, and slow moving lines certainly don't create that.

Another reason might be a lineup change or development that wasn't accounted for in the original number. A player like Albert Pujols can be worth twenty-five cents on the line. If he is out of the lineup, you'll see the odds on St. Louis move quickly to reflect his absence.

But the main reason a sports book will move the line is just plain old cash. If the current line is creating one way action, the book gives the unpopular team a more attractive price. Sometimes it happens quickly; betting groups will make their large plays and create steam moves. Or the line can slowly drift one way as the general public gradually chooses the same side throughout the day.

THE MONEY LINE

The most common way to bet baseball is using the money line. The money line is simply the odds on which team will win the game. In this way, baseball is different from football and basketball in the betting world. While bookmakers can use point spreads to even things out between two basketball teams, the low number of runs in a baseball game usually eliminates the possibility. This simplifies things for most bettors. Just pick the winner, and you win the money.

Knowing how to read the line is important, however. A bettor who consistently risks $180 to win $100 has to win over 64% of his wagers simply to break even. The underdog backer, betting $100 to win $170, just has to win 37% of the time to make his money back.

It is that needed win percentage that makes betting on heavy favorites so gruesome. At times, I will risk money on those "sure things". If I believe a team has an 80% chance of winning a game and it only costs me -$180, I'll close my eyes and pull the trigger. But I'm not happy about it. It is boring when you win, and execrable when you lose.

The table below shows the shows the true line on a team depending on its chances of winning the game.

TRUE LINE/ WIN PERCENTAGE TABLE

WIN %	TRUE LINE	WIN %	T LINE	WIN %	T LINE
25%	$3.00	45%	$1.22	65%	-$1.86
26%	$2.85	46%	$1.17	66%	-$1.94
27%	$2.70	47%	$1.13	67%	-$2.03
28%	$2.57	48%	$1.08	68%	-$2.13
29%	$2.45	49%	$1.04	69%	-$2.23
30%	$2.33	50%	$1.00	70%	-$2.33
31%	$2.23	51%	-$1.04	71%	-$2.45
32%	$2.13	52%	-$1.08	72%	-$2.57
33%	$2.03	53%	-$1.13	73%	-$2.70
34%	$1.94	54%	-$1.17	74%	-$2.85
35%	$1.86	55%	-$1.22	75%	-$3.00
36%	$1.78	56%	-$1.27	76%	-$3.17
37%	$1.70	57%	-$1.33	77%	-$3.35
38%	$1.63	58%	-$1.38	78%	-$3.55
39%	$1.56	59%	-$1.44	79%	-$3.76
40%	$1.50	60%	-$1.50	80%	-$4.00

41%	$1.44	61%	-$1.56	81%	-$4.26
42%	$1.38	62%	-$1.63	82%	-$4.56
43%	$1.33	63%	-$1.70	83%	-$4.88
44%	$1.27	64%	-$1.78	84%	-$5.25

To bettors who make their own line and like to translate a team's expected winning percentage into its own true line, the process is simple:

Favorite line:
((1-expected win percentage) / expected win percentage) * -1

If a team has a 60% chance of winning, the formula will look like this:
((1-60%) / 60%) * -1 = -1.50 line.

On underdogs, the formula is reversed and no negative number needed:
40% / (1-40%) = 1.50 true line.

DECIMAL ODDS

European sports books use decimal odds rather than the "American" type of line. A -110 favorite would be listed as a 1.91 favorite. Decimal odds are also easier to work with if you know how to calculate the conversion:

For underdog conversions to decimal odds: (money line/100) + 1
For favorite conversions: 1 - (100/money line)

For decimal odds of 2.00 or higher: money line = (decimal - 1) *100
For decimal odds less than 2.00: money line = (-100)/(decimal -1)

THE RUN LINE

Everyone loved the Red Sox in Game One of the 2007 World Series. On the mound for Boston was one of the best pitchers in baseball, right hander Josh Beckett. Lefty Jeff Francis took the mound for Colorado. The Rockies were sizzling, seemingly not losing since May or so. But that hot streak had a price. Colorado hadn't played in eight days, and many believed the layoff would make the team rusty. Boston was -215 favorites going into the game.

It was a steep price to pay for the right side. Many bettors, me included, have a rather unhealthy aversion to betting heavy favorites. To those of us with this handicap, the friendly bookies have thrown us a bone. The Run Line is a form of point spread in baseball. Instead of simply picking the winner of the game, a bettor can trade a run for some extra dollar value on the bet. In other words, you can bet the Red Sox will win by more than one run. In exchange, the odds move in your favor. If Boston wins by only one run, you lose the bet. Good play? Sometimes it is, sometimes it isn't. In this case, I took Beckett and the Red Sox -1.5 for -110. It wasn't even close. Boston scored three in the first for an early lead and put the game away for good with a seven run outburst in the 5th inning. The Red Sox beat the rusty Rockies 13-1.

Historically, a single run wins about 27.7% of all games. This number, however, needs to be separated into home games and road games. Road teams are more likely to win by more than one run because they will get nine chances to score in a game. If the road team is winning by one run in the ninth inning, they keep hitting. Not true for home teams. Over the last eight years, 31.5% of all home wins have been by one run. In comparison, only 23.4% of all road wins have been by one run. The difference is real, and sports books make this adjustment when setting the Run Line.

Sports books also adjust the run line according to the Over/Under line. The more runs expected to be scored in a game, the less likely the game will result in a one-run victory for either team. The table below shows three years' worth of data:

ROAD TEAM

O/U	Rd Wins	1 Run Wins	1 RUN WINS	WIN > 1
7	41.8%	31.0%	12.9%	28.9%
7.5	43.6%	24.0%	10.5%	33.1%
8	48.5%	28.2%	13.7%	34.8%
8.5	46.6%	23.8%	11.1%	35.5%
9	45.5%	22.2%	10.1%	35.4%

9.5	44.3%	23.8%	10.5%	33.7%
10	49.4%	26.2%	12.9%	36.5%
10.5	43.4%	20.3%	8.8%	34.6%
11	43.7%	20.3%	8.9%	34.8%
11.5	56.3%	19.4%	10.9%	45.3%
12	50.0%	23.5%	11.8%	38.2%
12.5	45.9%	24.1%	11.1%	34.9%

HOME TEAM

O/U	Hm WINS	% 1 Run W	1 RUN WIN	WIN> 1
7	58.2%	38.5%	22.4%	35.8%
7.5	56.4%	36.7%	20.7%	35.7%
8	51.5%	33.1%	17.0%	34.5%
8.5	53.4%	30.5%	16.3%	37.1%
9	54.5%	30.6%	16.7%	37.8%
9.5	55.7%	30.8%	17.1%	38.6%
10	50.6%	27.7%	14.0%	36.6%
10.5	56.6%	27.4%	15.5%	41.1%
11	56.3%	31.5%	17.7%	38.6%
11.5	43.8%	28.6%	12.5%	31.3%
12	50.0%	41.2%	20.6%	29.4%

When the total is listed at seven runs or less, 31% of all road wins are by one run. At 11 or more, only 20% of all road wins are by one run. The same holds true for home teams. When the home team wins a game whose total is seven runs, 38.5% of those victories are by only one run.

Generally speaking, a road team on the run line is worth about 55 to 60 cents. A home team is about 85 cents higher on the run line. With a lower total, that number will be higher; a higher total, it will be lower.

Most bettors use run lines to knock down heavy favorites to a decent number. However, the frustration having the team you bet on win by only one run can take a toll on a bettor. One method to avoid this disaster is to split your bet between the money line and run line. Let's say Boston is a -133 favorite on the road at Oakland. Instead of betting $100 on the Red Sox using the run line, I would bet:

- $55 on Boston to win $41
- $41 on New York -1.5 runs to win $51

If Boston loses, I'm out $96. If Boston wins by more than one run, I'm up $92. If Boston wins by one run, I break even. By manipulating bets this way, a bettor can get Boston – 1 for -$104.

This is my favorite way to bet medium to heavy favorites. I don't pay a lot of extra juice, and I still have my money on the team I want. Breaking even when my team wins by just one run keeps the pain away.

Another option open for bettors is to take an underdog on the plus side of the run line. Instead of giving up 1.5 runs, a gambler would collect if his team won outright or lost by just one run. Few recreational bettors take this play; I dislike it simply because I like collecting the juicy payoffs when an underdog wins the game. It is something I look at on each game, however. The public overwhelmingly takes favorites on the run line, occasionally pushing up the value on the other side high enough for me to take a stab at it.

Sports books generally follow these guidelines when it comes to setting a run line price:

Home		Line	Away	Run	Line
-200	-1.5	-105	-200	-1.5	-130
-190	-1.5	100	-190	-1.5	-125
-180	-1.5	105	-180	-1.5	-120
-170	-1.5	110	-170	-1.5	-115
-160	-1.5	120	-160	-1.5	-110
-150	-1.5	130	-150	-1.5	100
-140	-1.5	140	-140	-1.5	110
-130	-1.5	150	-130	-1.5	120
-120	-1.5	160	-120	-1.5	130
-110	-1.5	170	-110	-1.5	135

One other betting option is the alternate run line. The alternate run line handicaps the dog by 1.5 runs. A +200 underdog may be a +500 underdog minus the 1.5 runs. At one time, taking the alternate run line was lucrative. The lines tightened up, however, and the betting opportunities weren't quite as evident. It is something to keep in mind though. There are still a lot of instances where taking the underdog –1.5 is profitable.

TOTALS

When you think of "key numbers" in handicapping, football and the number three comes immediately to mind. In baseball totals, those key numbers are seven and nine. A Chicago-St. Louis game in 2007 illustrates this fact. Carlos Zambrano and Adam Wainwright were on the mound. Both pitchers struggled in April, and the over/under line opened up at 8.5. I waited though. I liked the Under and was hoping to see the number rise once the betting public looked at the weather forecast (wind blowing out) and considered the recent form of both pitchers.

It is a good thing I did. The bettors loved the Over. Heavy action on the Over pushed the line to nine runs, a significant move. Sports books don't like moving on or off nine runs. The chart below detailing the number of runs scored in each game will give an indication as to why:

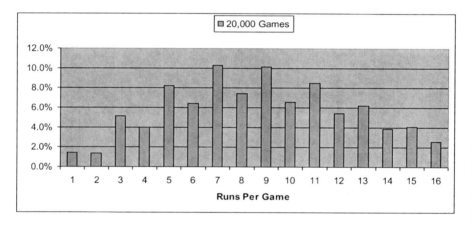

More games land on seven, nine, and 11 runs than any other number. The reason is simple: a tie game requires at least one more run to score before it ends. A game tied at four in the late innings more often than not will end with nine runs scored in the game, just like 3-3 games will usually end with a 4-3 victory from one team.

It is vital to get on the right side of these key numbers. If I like the Over in a game and the overnight total is at 8.5 runs, I make an immediate play. Waiting until the next day, in the hopes of seeing that total drop to eight runs, is simply not worth the risk of seeing it rise up to nine. To put it into perspective: 54.9% of all baseball games end up with nine or more runs scored in a game. 55.7% of all baseball games also end up with nine or less runs scored per game. By hook or by crook, I pull out all my tricks to get on the right side of nine when betting my totals.

Up to a point, however. Getting on the right side of nine has a price, and if it is too expensive then I'll just take what I can get. As I said earlier, many sports books don't like moving off the key numbers. For this reason, I'll sometimes see one book with a total of nine and another with a total of 9.5. The sports books that don't adjust the total will simply adjust the price: if I want the Under 9.5, I pay more than if I want the under nine runs.

But how much more should I pay and what is the right price? One common question when playing totals is the value of a half run. Data from the last three years tells us that games land on nine when the total is nine about 11% of the time. In other words:

- Bettor A playing over nine runs can be expected to win 44.5% of the time, lose 44.5%, and push 11% of the time. Since he has a 50/50 shot at winning, the Over/Under nine line should be -110.

- Bettor B playing Over 8.5 runs can be expected to win 55.5% of the time, and lose just 44.5%. Using those odds plus the sports book vigorish, the Over 8.5 line should be -135.

Over nine runs (-110) is equal to Over 8.5 runs (-135). The half run going from 8.5 to nine is worth about 25 cents. A table containing the value of a half run off each number is listed on the next page:

Total #1	Total #2	Price
7.5	7	34 cents
8.5	8	19 cents
9.5	9	25 cents
10.5	10	17 cents
11.5	11	29 cents

The decision to wait on betting the Under in the Chicago-St. Louis paid off as the Cubs beat up on Wainwright and the Cardinals 8-1. Understanding totals, and the key numbers to dance around, will often allow you to 'steal' a bet while others on the same side have losing tickets.

FIFTH INNING WAGERS

It looked over when Mariano Riviera entered the game early in the season in 2007. One of the greatest closers in baseball history, Riviera had some breathing room with a 4-2 Yankees lead against Oakland. The A's were struggling on offense, and when Riviera quickly got two outs the conclusion to the game seemed clear. A Todd Walker single extended the game. Jason Kendall then walked, bringing Marco Scutaro up representing the winning run. The end was crushing to Yankees' backers. The three run homer to left field gave the A's a shocking 5-4 win, sending the game over the total as well. For me, it was a double whammy. I had already started counting my chickens, and what could have been a decent day turned into a disaster.

Nothing is more frustrating than a late inning lead being blown by a shaky bullpen. It isn't a common occurrence, but wasted games can damage more than just a bettor's bankroll. The psychological aspects of losing a game that was thought to have been in the bag can carry over far beyond just that night's games.

One way to combat this is the use of fifth inning bets. Fifth inning bets are simply wagers on which team will be leading after five innings. Like the run line, prop bets like this were at one time relatively useless: the vigorish charged was too expensive to make these bets profitable over the long term.

Pinnaclesports.com has changed the equation, however. Just as run lines can now be used as effectively as money line wagers, so can fifth inning wagers. Pinnacle uses a dime line in both fifth inning side bets and totals. The April 25 game between Atlanta/Milwaukee provides a good example detailing the potential profits of fifth inning bets:

TEAM	5TH INNING	GAME LINE
ATLANTA	-1.19	-1.17
MILWAUKEE	+1.09	+1.09

An Atlanta bettor would pay just two extra cents by making a fifth inning wager vs. the entire game. Considering how unreliable the Braves bullpen can be, many bettors will find it comforting to bet the fifth inning rather than the entire game. Some might make half a bet for the fifth inning and half for the game. The blown saves, painful still, are a bit easier to take.

At least that is the perception. The question remains; how often will these bets actually cut a bettor's losses? Using five years' worth of data and ignoring fifth inning ties, we can determine how such a strategy works:

	5TH INN WIN	GAME
ROAD	46.5%	46.2%
HOME	53.5%	53.8%

A bettor splitting his wagers on the fifth inning and the complete game would show a slight improvement. That improvement, however, is unlikely to result in higher profits. The ability to shop for the best lines is virtually nil in fifth inning bets; only Pinnacle and Bet Jamaica offer the dime line (5Dimes does offer a 15-cent line that sometimes has value). This lack of line variety means you are stuck with whatever line is dealt, unlike complete game wagers.

The data can be broken down a bit further:

ROAD WINS BOTH	37.2%
ROAD WINS 5TH, HOME WINS GAME	9.3%
HOME WINS BOTH	44.8%
HOME WINS 5TH, ROAD WINS GAME	8.7%

About 18% of all games will see a team losing after five innings come back to win the game. One piece of conventional wisdom in baseball is that home teams are more likely to stage comebacks due to crowd support and momentum; I don't buy that argument. Road teams will blow a few more games than home teams. The difference, however, isn't substantial (about 10-12 games each season).

So what teams are most likely to lose fifth inning leads? Common sense would say teams with a poor bullpen. This was the case in 2007:

TEAM	BLOWN LEADS	BULLPEN ERA	PEN RANK
TAMPA BAY	19	6.16	30
BALTIMORE	16	5.71	29
WHITE SOX	18	5.47	28
CINCINNATI	24	5.10	27
PITTSBURGH	13	4.77	26

While bad teams are bad for a variety of reasons, bullpens usually play a major factor. The next time you look at betting the juicy money lines that are permanently attached to such teams, consider the fifth inning wagers. The price is almost as nice, and you won't have the dregs of the bullpen

FACTORING FOR PLATOON SPLITS

The theory of platooning has gone through various stages over the years. In 1914, the Red Sox won a World Series thanks to its platoon system. Many major league baseball teams saw the effect and followed suit. Platooning gradually began to fade out around the peak of the Babe Ruth years for a variety of reasons, chief among them resistance from players. Not until Casey Stengel was hired in New York did the platoon system become back in vogue. Earl Weaver started keeping detailed records of pitcher/hitter matchups, and made players like John Lowenstein and Elrod Hendricks into productive major league hitters. Tony LaRussa has taken it even further, keeping numerous left-handed pitchers in the bullpen solely to take advantage of the lefty-lefty matchups that favor pitchers.

Winning bettors understand this and take it into account when making plays. However, just as there is a risk in ignoring platoon splits, there is also a big risk in over-adjusting for it as well. The platoon factor is real; almost all right-handed hitters hit better against lefties than they do against right-handed pitchers. The same holds true on the other side of the plate as well; lefties hit better against their opposite number compared to how well they do against fellow left-handers.

These differences can be measured relatively accurately. RH batters historically hit 9% better against lefties than versus righties. This number has been constant for 50 plus years. Hitters who may have pounded lefties for one season will likely revert back to this 9% spread the next season. A right-handed hitter's platoon splits has no predictive value for the next season. If you want to find out how well a RH batter will hit lefties, the best way is to determine how he hits righties.

LH batters are a bit different. Whereas right-handed hitters who can't hit RH pitchers are weeded out of baseball in the minor leagues, many left-handed hitters are able to advance through the system without facing a lot of high quality left-handed pitchers. Some learn how to hit them, and others don't. Unlike RH batters, there are very large, persistent platoon splits among some lefties. It is important to note which team is loaded with left-handed batters and check their platoon splits. It is these teams that are more vulnerable to a platoon effect than teams more 'righty-centric'.

There were a handful of teams that had exploitable splits in 2009. The Orioles had major problems against lefties. The Cardinals likewise were much better against righties compared to lefties. The White Sox had the opposite split, pounding left-handed pitching while having big problems versus righties, in large part because they were loaded with right handed hitters. The tables below shows each team's platoon splits for the 2009 season:

Team	Arm	AB	HR	BA	OBP	SLG	OPS
Arizona	LHers	1429	50	.243	.329	.412	.741
Arizona	RHers	4136	123	.257	.323	.419	.742

Arizona was just 17-30 last year against left-handed starters, but the stats show that its offense was equally effective against lefthanders and righties. The signing of Adam LaRoche helps keep the Diamondbacks lineup balanced, although the question marks surrounding Connor Jackson's health are worrisome. The lineup against right-handers is pretty well set. Against lefties, however, it is still up in the air. Stephen Drew is awful against lefties so he won't likely be batting leadoff against lefties. On paper at least, Arizona has plenty of depth to cover up any platoon weaknesses.

Team	Arm	AB	HR	BA	OBP	SLG	OPS
Atlanta	LHers	1672	48	.268	.339	.411	.750
Atlanta	RHers	3867	101	.261	.339	.403	.742

The Braves won 59% of their games against lefties in 2009 but like Arizona, the stats show there wasn't much of a difference with the bats. The signing of Troy Glaus should help keep the Braves strong against lefties, while the addition of Jason Heyward to the outfield mix with Matt Diaz and Melky Cabrera will add balance to the lineup. It helps having a switch-hitter like Chipper Jones in the lineup as well.

Team	Arm	AB	HR	BA	OBP	SLG	OPS
Baltimore	LHers	1950	43	.255	.317	.374	.691
Baltimore	RHers	3668	117	.276	.340	.437	.777

Baltimore was awful against lefthanders last season, batting just .255 with a .691 OPS. Adam Jones and Matt Wieters will have another year's worth of experience, however, and the addition of Miguel Tejada, Garrett Atkins and switch-hitter Cesar Izturis will help.

Team	Arm	AB	HR	BA	OBP	SLG	OPS
Boston	LHers	1627	62	.274	.359	.453	.812
Boston	RHers	3916	150	.268	.349	.454	.803

One thing you can always assume about the current Red Sox management: they know when they have a weakness. Boston signed RH hitters Marco Scutaro, Adrian Beltre and Mike Cameron in the offseason, and have JD Drew, Victor Martinez, Jacoby Ellsbury and David Ortiz swinging from the left side. Mike Lowell and Jeremy Hermida are around to help out either off the bench or in a platoon as well. Overall, their offense will be down this year. The defense is much improved, however. In 2009, Boston went 30-26 against lefties (-8.4 units) and 65-44 vs. RHers (+9.8).

Team	Arm	AB	HR	BA	OBP	SLG	OPS
W-Sox	LHers	1470	56	.282	.353	.448	.800
W-Sox	RHers	3993	128	.249	.320	.398	.718

The White Sox did much better against lefthanders in 2009, thanks to a lineup loaded with right-handed hitters like Alexei Ramirez, Konerko, Beckham, and Carlos Quentin. Against lefties, Chicago was 25-24 while just 54-59 vs. RHers. The White Sox added LH bats like Mark Teahen and Juan Pierre, but neither strike fear in right-handed pitchers. Expect more struggles vs. RHers in 2010.

Team	Arm	AB	HR	BA	OBP	SLG	OPS
Cubs	LHers	1082	25	.251	.331	.388	.720
Cubs	RHers	4404	136	.256	.332	.411	.743

The Cubs should have two left-handed hitters in their lineup in 2010: Mike Fontenot and Kosuke Fukudome. That doesn't bode well for Chicago against RH pitching, but the Cubs have been doing this for a few years now. Chicago won 52% of its games against righties (but lost 13.1 units) compared to 50% of games in which left-handed pitchers started (-.4 units).

Team	Arm	AB	HR	BA	OBP	SLG	OPS
Reds	LHers	1346	35	.260	.324	.398	.722
Reds	RHers	4116	123	.243	.316	.393	.708

There isn't a lot of punch in the Reds lineup but on the plus side: the punch is lefty/righty balanced. Despite having a higher OPS against lefties, the Reds were just 19-25 against LH starters. When a right-hander is on the mound, Cincinnati went 59-59.

Team	Arm	AB	HR	BA	OBP	SLG	OPS
Cleveland	LHers	1387	44	.260	.342	.422	.765
Cleveland	RHers	4181	117	.265	.338	.415	.753

Cleveland should have plenty of left-handed bats in the lineup in 2010; six of the nine projected starters for the Indians are either switch-hitters or left-handed batters. That should help their record out versus righties: the Indians were just 48-74 in games started by right-handed pitchers.

Team	Arm	AB	HR	BA	OBP	SLG	OPS
Colorado	LHers	1586	56	.253	.335	.430	.765
Colorado	RHers	3812	134	.264	.346	.445	.791

The Rockies were much better against right-handed starters, winning 17.7 units with a 65-44 record. Lefties gave them a little more trouble: Colorado lost 4.6 units with a 28-29 record. Colorado still comes into the 2010 loaded with left-handed bats. Only Troy Tulowitzki offers right-handed pop for the Rockies.

Team	Arm	AB	HR	BA	OBP	SLG	OPS
Detroit	LHers	1471	52	.259	.341	.426	.768
Detroit	RHers	4069	131	.261	.327	.413	.740

What do Miguel Cabrera, Brandon Inge, Magglio Ordonez, Gerald Laird, Scott Sizemore, Ray Rayburn, and Adam Everett all have in common? All are expected to start for the Tigers in 2010, and all are right-handed batters. Only Carlos Guillen (switch-hitter) will hit from the left side of the plate. Detroit was +6.2 units against lefties while just 57-57 vs. right-handers.

Team	Arm	AB	HR	BA	OBP	SLG	OPS
Florida	LHers	1514	42	.262	.329	.405	.734
Florida	RHers	4058	117	.270	.344	.420	.764

The Marlins were much better against right-handed pitchers in 2009, but that didn't show up on the money-line. Florida won just 2.1 units vs. RHers while winning +6.9 units when a left-handed pitcher was on the mound.

Team	Arm	AB	HR	BA	OBP	SLG	OPS
Houston	LHers	1210	36	.276	.323	.432	.755

Houston	RHers	4226	106	.256	.318	.391	.709

The Astros were heavy on right-handed hitters thanks to the likes of Carlos Lee, Miguel Tejada, Hunter Pence and Ty Wigginton. Tejada and Wigginton are gone, but Pedro Feliz and Jeff Keppinger will keep the Astros strong against left-handers. Lance Berkman, Michael Bourn and Kaz Matsui are the left-handed bats. That explains the difficulty Houston has vs. righties.

Team	Arm	AB	HR	BA	OBP	SLG	OPS
Royals	LHers	1770	39	.267	.328	.399	.727
Royals	RHers	3762	105	.255	.314	.408	.722

Kansas City had an awful record against LHers last year, but the numbers say there were other factors involved besides hitting. Maybe Zack Greinke didn't pitch when the opposing team had a lefty on the mound. The Royals have signed some new bodies to fill in the lineup, but none should make much of an impact.

Team	Arm	AB	HR	BA	OBP	SLG	OPS
LA Angels	LHers	1631	55	.286	.342	.446	.788
LA Angels	RHers	3991	118	.285	.353	.440	.793

The Angels were solid facing lefties and righties in 2009, with little difference in their overall hitting stats. They did have a great deal of success against LH starters, winning 66% of their games for +15.2 units. LH bat Hideki Matsui replaces Vlad Guerrero in the lineup, so that number is unlikely to continue in 2010.

Team	Arm	AB	HR	BA	OBP	SLG	OPS
Dodgers	LHers	1318	38	.272	.359	.427	.786
Dodgers	RHers	4274	107	.270	.342	.407	.748

The Dodgers were much better statistically vs. LH pitchers in 2009, but the numbers didn't translate to a good record. LA was just 27-23 vs. lefties and 72-48 facing right-handed starters. The Dodgers have been handcuffed financially in the off-season and didn't do much, so expect that 2009 trend to continue in 2010.

Team	Arm	AB	HR	BA	OBP	SLG	OPS

Team	Arm	AB	HR	BA	OBP	SLG	OPS
Brewers	LHers	1175	43	.270	.359	.449	.807
Brewers	RHers	4335	139	.261	.336	.420	.756

Prince Fielder is the only left-handed power bat in the lineup for the Brewers so there it is no surprise that Milwaukee were much better vs. LHers than righties. Milwaukee won 3.4 units against left-handed starters as opposed to losing 8.1 units when a right-hander was on the mound. Expect more of the same in 2010.

Team	Arm	AB	HR	BA	OBP	SLG	OPS
Twins	LHers	1783	52	.285	.344	.441	.785
Twins	RHers	3825	120	.269	.345	.423	.768

With Morneau and Mauer both lefties, one would expect the Twins to be struggle against left-handed pitchers. Statistically that wasn't the case. Record-wise, it was however. The Twins were just 28-34 vs. lefties and 59-45 against righties. Jim Thome's addition at DH isn't going to help vs. left-handers.

Team	Arm	AB	HR	BA	OBP	SLG	OPS
NY Mets	LHers	1374	34	.273	.336	.421	.757
NY Mets	RHers	4079	61	.269	.335	.385	.720

The Mets have added Jason Bay and Gary Matthews Jr. and lost Carlos Beltran for the beginning of the season. Francoeur and Wright will punish left-handed pitchers but there isn't any pop from the left-handed bats in the lineup.

Team	Arm	AB	HR	BA	OBP	SLG	OPS
Yankees	LHers	1714	76	.286	.365	.480	.846
Yankees	RHers	3946	168	.282	.360	.476	.837

The Yankees crushed everyone last season; it will likely continue in 2010 as well. Johnny Damon is gone but Nick Johnson and Curtis Granderson will make up the difference.

Team	Arm	AB	HR	BA	OBP	SLG	OPS
Oakland	LHers	1592	34	.251	.323	.372	.695
Oakland	RHers	3992	101	.267	.331	.407	.738

Oakland was horrible vs. left-handers last year, both statistically and on the money line. The A's were just 19-31 (-8.4 units) against LH starters and 56-56 (+11.4 units) vs. righties. Off-season changes haven't fixed this problem for Oakland.

Team	Arm	AB	HR	BA	OBP	SLG	OPS
Phillies	LHers	1518	68	.248	.335	.452	.787
Phillies	RHers	4060	156	.262	.334	.445	.779

The Phillies' big name players are left-handed hitters, but Jayson Werth and switch-hitters Jimmy Rollins and Shane Victorino help keep things in balance. The Phillies were +9.5 units versus LH starters while losing -5.2 against righties.

Team	Arm	AB	HR	BA	OBP	SLG	OPS
Pittsburgh	LHers	1435	34	.245	.307	.376	.683
Pittsburgh	RHers	3982	91	.254	.322	.391	.713

The Pirates only faced a left-handed starter 44 times in 2009, going 18-26 for negative 2.9 units. Pittsburgh went 44-73 against RH starters, good for a whopping -2.2 units. The lineup hasn't changed, so expect a long summer in Pittsburgh.

Team	Arm	AB	HR	BA	OBP	SLG	OPS
San Diego	LHers	1657	39	.236	.313	.363	.676
San Diego	RHers	3768	102	.245	.324	.389	.713

LH batter Adrian Gonzalez is the only power bat in the Padres lineup, so it is expected that a good left-hander will give San Diego fits. Gonzalez is on the trade block in 2010 so it is impossible to say what the splits will be for the Padres.

Team	Arm	AB	HR	BA	OBP	SLG	OPS
Giants	LHers	1325	33	.248	.301	.386	.687
Giants	RHers	4168	89	.26	.312	.390	.702

For the second year in a row, the Giants had more success in the win column versus RHers. Their offensive production wasn't that much better, however. Maybe Tim Lincecum pitched only when a righty was on the mound last year.

Team	Arm	AB	HR	BA	OBP	SLG	OPS
Seattle	LHers	1794	56	.255	.315	.407	.723
Seattle	RHers	3749	104	.260	.313	.399	.712

The Mariners have added switch-hitters Chone Figgins and Milton Bradley to the lineup this year, as well as acquiring Casey Kotchman to fill their first base hole. In 2009, Seattle was +13.7 units vs. RHers and -1.2 units against lefties, proof once again that over-reliance on a team's splits can be deadly.

Team	Arm	AB	HR	BA	OBP	SLG	OPS
St. Louis	LHers	1452	35	.233	.312	.362	.674
St. Louis	RHers	4013	125	.273	.340	.434	.774

The Cardinals were much better against RHers last season, but that didn't translate in the win-loss record. St. Louis went 63-51 vs. righties (-.5 units) and 28-23 against LHers (-1.8 units).

Team	Arm	AB	HR	BA	OBP	SLG	OPS
Rays	LHers	1724	58	.260	.353	.439	.791
Rays	RHers	3738	141	.264	.338	.440	.778

Tampa Bay has a well-balanced lineup, although a comeback season for Carlos Pena will help the Rays handle right-handed pitching. The Rays were 30-30 vs. lefties compared to 54-48 against righties.

Team	Arm	AB	HR	BA	OBP	SLG	OPS
Texas	LHers	1585	64	.257	.318	.440	.758
Texas	RHers	3941	160	.261	.320	.447	.767

The Rangers added Vladimir Guerrero over the off-season and have switch-hitter Justin Smoak ready to go in AAA, so expect Texas to be strong against left-handed pitching. The Rangers were +11.4 units last year vs. righties.

Team	Arm	AB	HR	BA	OBP	SLG	OPS
Toronto	LHers	1506	53	.261	.328	.431	.759
Toronto	RHers	4190	156	.268	.334	.444	.778

The Blue Jays made a big trade to acquire minor leaguer Brett Wallace this off-season, but he is expected to open up the season in AAA. The lineup will have a very familiar look to it; John Buck is expected to be the only new starter for Toronto.

Team	Arm	AB	HR	BA	OBP	SLG	OPS
Nationals	LHers	1206	32	.262	.351	.403	.754
Nationals	RHers	4287	124	.257	.332	.407	.739

Washington struggled versus right-handers last year, no surprise when your only worthwhile left-handed bat is Adam Dunn. Pudge Rodriguez and Adam Kennedy are the big acquisitions for the Nationals this year; expect more struggles this season. Washington was 49-80 vs. right-handers compared to a 10-23 record against lefties in 2010.

"Pitchers' platoon splits can be reliably measured much more easily than those of right- or left-handed hitters. A right-handed pitcher's platoon split is reasonably accurate once he has around 700 plate appearances against left-handed hitters; for a lefty, the number is about 450."

Tom Tango, Mitchell Litchtman, and Andrew Dolphin; page 160, The Book

INTERLEAGUE PLAY

It used to be rather simple in baseball. The National League is the National League, the American League is the American League, and never the twain shall meet. At least until the World Series. That all went out the window in 1997. Bud Selig and his cabal decided the game needed some spice to recover from the strike, and interleague play was it.

In the early years of play, bragging rights were hard to come by. By the end of the 2004 season, the American League had won 959 games while the NL won 988.

The American League has begun asserting its dominance in recent years, however. The AL has won 56% of interleague games since the beginning of the 2005 season. While this hasn't translated into World Champions (each league has won the Series twice since then), it still clearly indicates that the America League is the stronger league at this moment. The chart below shows the records since interleague play started in 1997:

YEAR	AL	NL	WIN %
1997	97	117	.453
1998	114	110	.509
1999	116	135	.462
2000	136	115	.542
2001	132	120	.524
2002	123	129	.488
2003	115	137	.456
2004	126	125	.502
2005	136	116	.540
2006	154	98	.611
2007	137	115	.544
2008	149	103	.591
2009	137	114	.546
TOTAL	1672	1534	.522

Recently there has been a generic rule of thumb that says the American League is about .35 or .40 runs better than the National League. A quick translation shows that a handicapper should add about 20 cents to his line to account for the domination of the AL over the NL. That might be a little high, but it is probably best to take it on a case by case basis.

There is another variable added to the handicapping puzzle during interleague games. One must account for the rivalry factors in certain series. The Yankees vs. Mets mean a lot more to the teams and fans than a typical Mets-Nationals series. Pay close attention to bullpen use. Many managers may push their top relievers a little harder in order to grab a win against its rivals.

Some bettors love betting interleague games. They feel the added variables mean the lines are softer, and hence, more beatable. Others stay far away, unable to get a "feel" for the games and not willing to bet. I like it because shakes things up. However, adjustments need to be made in order to have success.

2009 Interleague Record

Club	W	L	Win Pct	Club	W	L	Win Pct
Bal	11	7	.611	Ari	5	10	.333
Bos	11	7	.611	Atl	7	8	.467
Chw	11	6	.647	Chi	6	8	.429
Cle	5	13	.278	Cin	6	9	.400
Det	10	8	.556	Col	11	4	.733
KC	8	10	.444	Flo	10	8	.556
LAA	14	4	.778	Hou	6	9	.400
Min	12	6	.667	LAD	9	9	.500
NYY	10	8	.556	Mil	5	10	.333
Oak	5	13	.278	NYY	5	10	.333
Sea	11	7	.611	Phi	6	12	.333
Tam	13	5	.722	Pit	8	7	.533
Tex	9	9	.500	StL	5	10	.333
Tor	7	11	.389	SD	9	6	.600
				SF	9	6	.600
				Was	7	11	.389

WHEN TO BET THE GAMES

September games always are tricky. You have minor league call-ups, disinterested teams, and strange lines. With college football just getting started, most bookmakers focus their attention elsewhere. That seemed to have been the case on September 2nd, 2007. The St. Louis Cardinals opened up as -137 favorites against the Cincinnati Reds. The Cardinals had worked its way back into the division race and had Braden Looper on the mound against Bronson Arroyo. That seemed like a fair price.

It was a Sunday, however, and Sundays often have unique lineups. So I paid close attention to the pre-game lineups, and when I heard Albert Pujols was getting a day off I pounded the Reds pretty hard. Others followed suit, and by game time the line had dropped to St. Louis -112.

A Rick Ankiel home run ruined my bet as the Cardinals won 3-2. I wasn't too upset. I got a great bargain on a live underdog. Bettors taking the overnight line had to feel pretty lucky, however. They made their bets assuming Pujols would be in the lineup.

It all ended well for Cardinal backers, but that game illustrated the dangers of betting early. There is often an internal battle over which way the line will move and whether or not you should wait for a line movement in your favor. A bettor needs to use his own judgment and expertise to answer this. There are positives in getting your bet down early just as there are positives in waiting until game time before making your plays

Each bet is an exercise in decision-making. With every decision, the longer you wait the more information you have. The main difficulty in decision-making is uncertainty. This uncertainty is often reduced in baseball once you discover who the umpire will be, who is in the starting lineup, if any key players are banged up, what the bullpen situation may be, how the weather will be, and so on. The more you know about a game the more you can measure the risk in comparison to the likelihood of success. Risk changes with each new development. It often is in the bettor's best interests to wait for as much information as a man could get.

Betting early has its rewards, however. You may not know everything that you will know tomorrow, but an early bettor will get more of a virgin line. The value has not been bet out of it. You also complete your work; the knowledge that you are done handicapping has some great psychological benefits. Burnout when betting baseball can easily occur. Betting early will help alleviate this potential.

It will also avoid other possible problems. There is a tendency in baseball to be bogged down in minutiae, or in looking for that perfect betting opportunity. It isn't too bright to spend 45 minutes in the mall parking lot waiting for the very best spot to park. It isn't too bright waiting for more information if you don't need it. There is a fine line between too little and too much information. That final piece of the puzzle is rarely needed to discover the picture. You might also ignore valuable news at the expense of the new stuff; early information that has an impact can be pushed out for more recent, inconsequential rumors.

There is no perfect time to place a bet on a game. Much depends on the process used to handicap, and your expectations regarding which way the line will move. Over time, an alert bettor will choose correctly more often than not. Keeping detailed notes regarding line movement helps as well

BETTING ON STREAKS

It seemed like a nothing game at the time. Colorado had just gotten blown out by the Florida Marlins at home, keeping the Rockies 6.5 games behind Arizona and mired in fourth place in the NL West. With just fourteen games left in the season, it looked like Colorado was toast.

Then they started winning. And winning. And winning. Rookie Franklyn Morales got the ball rolling with a shutout of Florida on September 16. A two-out, bottom of the 9th inning home run by Todd Helton capped off a double header sweep of the Dodgers and moved Colorado into a 3rd place tie with Los Angeles on September 18. Next was a series sweep of San Diego. Then another Dodgers series sweep. Two of three from Arizona to end the season. When the smoke cleared, Colorado had won thirteen of its final fourteen games to force a playoff game with San Diego for the Wild Card slot. The success continued in the 2007 post-season; the Rockies advanced to the World Series before getting swept by the Red Sox 4-0.

Streak bettors were ecstatic, and wealthy. Streak bettors operate under a simple theory. Baseball is a game of streaks. Find a team that is on a roll, pound that team while it is hot, and abandon ship once that streak ends. You only lose once using this method. But is it profitable?

It hasn't been recently. The table below shows how well teams on winnings streaks have done over the last four years:

Streak	Wins	Los	Profit
3	640	613	-3930
4	318	320	-5710
5	171	145	-1065
6	95	76	120
7	63	31	2280
8	27	34	-1820
9	13	14	-410
TOTAL	1327	1233	-10535

A $100 bettor would have lost $10,535 betting on those hot teams.

We can break it down into more subsets, however. How well do home favorites do when they are on a winning streak?

HOME FAVORITES

STREAK	RECORD	PROFIT
3	141-98	-1025
4	86-42	+2150
5	52-29	+615
6	29-20	-330
7	19-9	+345
8	11-6	+45
9	3-3	-170
10	1-1	-110

Total profit by betting on favored home teams when they are streaking: $1,520. By waiting until the fourth game to start betting the steaks, the bettor would have made $2,520. What about home underdogs?

HOME DOGS

STREAK	RECORD	PROFIT
3	36-54	-665
4	21-28	+25
5	7-10	-60
6	3-4	-75
7	1-0	+105
8	0-2	-200
9	0-1	-100

The net loss for home underdogs is -$970. Now to favorites playing on the road:

ROAD FAVORITES

STREAK	RECORD	PROFIT
3	71-52	-165
4	34-26	-670
5	21-14	-360
6	11-11	-520
7	10-3	+640
8	2-8	-925
9	2-2	-90
10	0-2	-320

Road favorites on a winning streak show a net loss of $1361. This time waiting until the fourth game of the winning streak doesn't matter; road favorites on hot streaks four games or more still lose $2245 on just 146 games. Road underdogs aren't much better:

ROAD UNDERDOGS

STREAK	RECORD	PROFIT
3	62-109	-2500
4	27-45	-620
5	17-18	+555
6	8-11	-145
7	6-3	+490
8	1-4	-210

Betting blindly on streaking road underdogs results in a loss of $2,270. Taking away teams on just a three game winning streak, however, and the results aren't so ugly. In 143 games, a bettor will realize a $230 profit.

Summing up the data: betting on streaking home favorites shows a profit. Home underdogs, away favorites, and away underdogs all are disasters waiting to happen, however. So much so, in fact, that one has to wonder how much the 15-unit profit on home favorites was simply a fluke. When playing streaks, tread cautiously. Momentum is nice to have, but baseball is often like craps. What happened yesterday often has little bearing on what happens today.

EARLY SEASON SCHEDULING ILLUSIONS

It was doom and gloom around the Yankees last May. Stuck with a 15-17 record after getting beat by Roy Halladay, the Yankees were 6.5 games behind the Red Sox. The tabloids were going nuts along with the rest of the country; all that money spent on Sabathia, Burnett and Teixeira was going up in smoke. Obviously that was forgotten in October. From that May 9th day, New York went 99-47 in rolling to the World Championship.

On the other side of the coin, there was the Kansas City Royals. We all now know the Royals as the pathetic 65-97 team that has embarrassed itself for the last 20 years. On May 9th, however, that awful team was in first place and looking like it could compete the rest of the year.

Typical early season flukes? Sure, up to a point. But the Yankees were also hurt by the schedule makers. Of their first 34 games, only 13 were at home in their new stadium. They opened the year with a nine-game road trip, not a good way to celebrate the opening of a new era. The Royals, on the other hand, had the majority of their games at home against lesser competition. They were playing decent baseball, but the schedule helped out as well.

When a team is getting a lot of publicity early in the season, make sure you check out the schedule. Should we expect the Yankees to struggle again starting out the 2010 season? They very well could. The Yankees have road games in 22 of their first 34 games next season. The Braves have a similar ratio of home games to road games to start off the season. Boston, on the other hand, plays most of their early season games at Fenway. The Mets and Astros also play a big chunk of their April games at home.

So if you hear wild joy and giddiness coming from Astros and Mets fans early in 2010, remember that the schedule is playing a role. Once things balance out, those April surprises aren't going to be so profitable.

HANDICAPPING THE MARKET

Some bettors handicap the teams, others handicap the market. Bettors who handicap the market pay little attention to whom is playing whom. They focus primarily on who is betting what. It is the Las Vegas version of "It's not what you know, it is who you know." These bettors spend all their effort studying line moves, trying to figure out what the sharp players are betting and tagging along.

There are some very vague assumptions that these "Steam players" make:

1) Professional wagers bet early
2) The public bets late
3) Early line moves tend to be sharp
4) Late line moves tend to be from the public
5) Extremely late line moves tend to come from sharps taking advantage of the late line moves from the public.

Steam bettors respect the early line moves and discount late moves. They have a rule of thumb that says to bet favorites early and wait until game time before betting dogs. I'm not sure if I buy that or not for baseball, but that's the philosophy in football and basketball. Sports books will often over-react to steam, moving the line too far off the "right number". At this time you may see these market handicappers jump back in, this time buying the opposite side of the sharp money at a much better price. The assumption here is that the initial lines makers know their stuff and the value has moved to the other side thanks to the steam.

LINES SERVICES

Vital to any steam chaser, lines services can save a bettor a great deal of hassle by keeping lines on most big sports books on one screen. Instead of logging in to a number of different sports books to get current odds, a bettor simply subscribes to a lines service. The first lines service was Don Best, formed in 1989 by Don Besssette before being sold to Al Corbo in 1992. Don Best initially featured lines from the Stardust, the Mirage, and the Riviera sports books in Las Vegas. The first offshore sports book was added in 1993. In 1997, the website was launched and Don Best immediately became a must have for sports books and major bettors.

Don Best has been sold several times in recent years, most recently to Big Stick Media in 2008. While still thought by many to be the best service available, its high cost ($499 a month) and history of poor customer service has opened the door to other lines services.

Most notable of these services is Sportsoptions.com. Sportsoptions premium service costs $299 a month and offers real time odds for the majority of sports books. The downside to Sportsoptions is it doesn't offer real-time odds to a handful of books, especially Bookmaker.com. Bookmaker has an exclusive agreement with Don Best and refuses to offer its live feeds to other services. While it is a must have out for a football and basketball bettor, it uses a 20 cent line for baseball, meaning a baseball bettor will very rarely find value at that book.

What makes Sportsoptions stand out in the lines service market is the injury reports. Sportsoptions has a team of employees on staff searching out game information and prides itself on being the first to announce injury news and lineup information. Information is money in sports betting, and being one of the first to know Albert Pujols is sitting out a game more than makes up the cost of a lines service.

A third quality line service is G and J Update out of Las Vegas. G and J was the first company to compete with the Don Best monster and one key reason why Don Best has lowered its prices in recent years. Smaller than Don Best and Sportsoptions, G and J's premium service is $200 a month.

There are also several other free live lines services on the internet. To a smaller bettor who doesn't chase steam, these appear work well enough. Baseball lines are relatively static, and the typical bettor will bet most of his action at the same handful of books.

It is the injury reports and lineup notices that set the premium lines services apart, however. If you plan on betting a lot of baseball, it is important to have one of the pay services. For my money, Sportsoptions is the best. But the other two work well also. All three offer a free trial period; if you wish to buy a service make sure you test all three out first.

THE HIDDEN VALUE OF BAD TEAMS

Betting on the great teams rarely make a bettor any money over the long term. Sports books know the public likes to back these teams and add a little to the price. A winner's tax, one may call it.

On September 1st last year, the most profitable team in baseball last season was the Angels. With a 78-52 record, the Angels were +21.6 units at that time. After that date? The Angels went 24-17 for -4.7 units.

The next most profitable team was the Texas Rangers (72-58, +16.5 units). Their record in September and October was 15-17, a loss of 5.2 units. The Dodgers were #3 (+12 units). After August, LA lost 3.6 units.

In total, there were five teams that had shown at least a 10 unit profit versus the money line through August 31st. All five of them lost money in September.

The opposite is true for bad teams, however. The public isn't going to bet the Padres of the world, no matter what the cost. This will move the line higher than it should be, creating value for the crap sandwich no one wants to bite.

A winning bettor has to be willing to bet these bad teams. This is especially true in baseball, where even the worst team has a decent shot at winning the game. The Royals, Reds, and Padres showed some life down the stretch last year. Keep an eye out for those types of teams.

That doesn't mean it is best to blindly bet these teams. Or even to give them the benefit of the doubt. Some teams will pack it in early; this was the case with Baltimore and Cleveland last year. When a team is melting down, stay far away.

MELTDOWNS

In most cases, it is silly to change power ratings of teams that hit a little slump or get on a hot streak. Streaks happen and over-reacting means a bettor will sell low and buy high. But some instances demand a change in perspective:

A) A team is losing consistently as a favorite.
B) A team's manager is under fire
C) A team is having problems with its fans and media
D) A team that was expected to contend for the division title is mired in a slump behind the leaders.

When teams are having these problems, it is time to wait it out before betting on them. The team should rebound, if they are playing beneath their level of talent. But there is no reason to ride them until they start showing a little life.

HOME FIELD ADVANTAGE

Home teams win about 58% of the time in the NFL. In the NHL, home teams win about 63%. Pro basketball sees its home fans go home happy around 60% of the time. Baseball doesn't have that huge advantage. On average, home teams win 54% of the time.

The advantage still has to be taken into account, however. The reasons for home field advantage are unclear: friendly fans, familiarity with a stadium's unique characteristics and umpiring bias towards the home team have all been mentioned as possible reasons a home team is better at home.

Whatever the reason, a bettor needs to account for this advantage. The typical bonus price for home field advantage is 16 to 18 cents. In other words, if two evenly matched teams were playing, the home team would be about a -117 favorite.

It is just a generic rule of thumb, however. As Bill James once said, an undefeated team has no home field advantage. What he meant is that home field advantage is simply the difference between how well a team plays at home and how well that same team plays on the road. That's where I focus most of my attention. By concentrating on the outliers, I can grind out a few more bets and avoid plays that my numbers would otherwise indicate as offering good value.

MINNESOTA

One of these outliers is Minnesota. The Twins historically have had one of the most powerful home field advantages in baseball. The Metrodome created a ton of problems for players, especially teams without experience dealing with the crowd and unique atmosphere. There is no way to tell how well the new Target Field will treat its home team. The field dimensions are similar to the Metrodome. But the natural grass, cold weather, and cozy confines of Target Field will be a different experience for fans and players both.

Year	Hm Win	Hm Loss	Win %	Units	Rd Win	Rd Loss	Win %	Units
2005	45	36	55.6%	-1	38	43	46.9%	-7.1
2006	54	29	65.1%	16.6	42	40	51.2%	1.9
2007	41	40	50.6%	-15.2	38	43	46.9%	-0.3
2008	53	28	65.4%	18.6	35	47	42.7%	-9.6
2009	49	34	59.0%	3.6	38	45	45.8%	-4.4
	242	167	59.2%	22.6	191	218	46.7%	-19.5

BALTIMORE

Baltimore finally had something resembling a home field advantage in 2009. They still weren't good in Camden Yards. They were just much worse on the road. Sports Illustrated did a poll in 2005 asking major league players for the most difficult place to play in baseball. 21% said Yankee Stadium. 20% said Fenway Park. Camden Yards? Nowhere to be found. At the end of the article was this blurb: "Every stadium except Camden Yards received at least one vote." The Orioles haven't earned a bonus for playing at home; until they do it is silly to give Baltimore the standard 17 cents home field advantage premium.

Year	Hm Win	Hm Loss	Win %	Units	Rd Win	Rd Loss	Win %	Units
2005	36	45	44.4%	-19.4	38	43	46.9%	8.9
2006	40	41	49.4%	-2.1	30	51	37.0%	-19
2007	35	46	43.2%	-15.5	34	47	42.0%	-11
2008	37	43	46.3%	-5.5	31	50	38.3%	-4.1
2009	39	42	48.1%	-4.3	25	56	30.9%	-9
	187	217	46.3%	-46.8	158	247	39.0%	-34

CHICAGO CUBS

One would think the Cubs and their idiot fans would make it hard for opposing teams to win at Wrigley. That usually wasn't the case until recent years. The Cubs weren't as dominant at home as they were in 2008, but they were still nine games better at home than on the road. Time will tell if they can keep up this performance. Either way, the bookie will typically make you pay out the nose if you want to bet the Cubs.

Year	Hm Win	Hm Loss	Win %	Units	Rd Win	Rd Loss	Win %	Units
2005	38	43	46.9%	-19.9	41	40	50.6%	4.1
2006	36	45	44.4%	-14	30	51	37.0%	-10.7
2007	44	38	53.7%	-11.3	41	42	49.4%	-4
2008	55	28	66.3%	8.8	42	39	51.9%	2
2009	46	34	57.5%	-6.4	37	44	45.7%	-10.3
	219	188	53.8%	-42.8	191	216	46.9%	-18.9

BOSTON

The Red Sox take full advantage of the unique characteristics of Fenway Park. In the past, Boston dominates at home while is just mediocre on the road. That trend continued in 2009. Despite winning 95 games, the Red Sox were five games below .500 on the road. That isn't an easy feat.

Year	Hm Win	Hm Loss	Win %	Units	Rd Win	Rd Loss	Win %	Units
2005	54	28	65.9%	10.6	41	42	49.4%	-9.7
2006	48	33	59.3%	4.1	38	43	46.9%	-8.2
2007	58	31	65.2%	6.6	49	38	56.3%	5.2
2008	58	28	67.4%	14.4	43	44	49.4%	-3.7
2009	56	26	68.3%	16	39	44	47.0%	-9.5
	274	146	65.2%	51.7	210	211	49.9%	-25.9

TAMPA BAY

Even when the Rays were bad, they were always solid at home. Teams that have a unique home park tend to have better home field advantage. Minnesota, Boston and Tampa are good examples of this. The Rays were an incredible 20 games better at home than on the road in 2009.

Year	Hm Win	Hm Loss	Win %	Units	Rd Win	Rd Loss	Win %	Units
2005	40	41	49.4%	9.1	27	54	33.3%	-6.3
2006	41	40	50.6%	10.9	20	61	24.7%	-29.3
2007	37	44	45.7%	-5.8	29	52	35.8%	-8.8
2008	62	27	69.7%	28.6	43	46	48.3%	-0.8
2009	52	29	64.2%	7.5	32	49	39.5%	-19.1
	232	181	56.2%	50.3	151	262	36.6%	-64.3

Complete home and away records for the rest of Major League baseball are listed on the following pages. To break up the monotony of endless tables, I have included charts of each team's home and away performance over the last five years. The charts detail the fluctuations of home field advantage from year to year. The dark line is the team's performance at home, while the lighter line is its winning percentage on the road. On average, the home team should average a difference of 7-8% from its road record.

Arizona

Team	Year	Hm Win	Hm Loss	Win %	Units	Rd Win	Rd Loss	Win %	Units
Arizona	2005	36	45	44.4%	-16.6	41	40	50.6%	10.5
Arizona	2006	39	42	48.1%	-7.6	37	44	45.7%	1.3
Arizona	2007	52	33	61.2%	12.8	41	43	48.8%	4.4
Arizona	2008	48	33	59.3%	1.6	34	47	42.0%	-16.9
Arizona	2009	36	44	45.0%	-15.9	34	48	41.5%	-7.8
Arizona Total		211	197	51.7%	-25.7	187	222	45.7%	-8.5

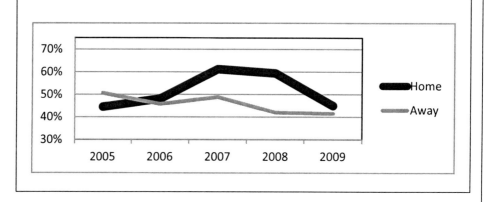

Atlanta

Team	Year	Hm Win	Hm Loss	Win %	Units	Rd Win	Rd Loss	Win %	Units
Atlanta	2005	54	29	65.1%	13.1	37	46	44.6%	-10.1
Atlanta	2006	40	41	49.4%	-13.9	39	42	48.1%	-3.4
Atlanta	2007	44	37	54.3%	-5.7	40	41	49.4%	-3
Atlanta	2008	43	38	53.1%	-4.7	29	52	35.8%	-19.1
Atlanta	2009	40	41	49.4%	-22.9	46	35	56.8%	12.2
Atlanta Total		221	186	54.3%	-34.1	191	216	46.9%	-23.4

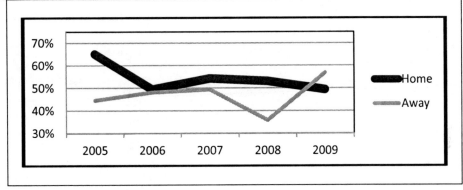

Chicago White Sox

Team	Year	Hm Win	Hm Loss	Win %	Units	Rd Win	Rd Loss	Win %	Units
White Sox	2005	52	35	59.8%	3.9	58	29	66.7%	30.9
White Sox	2006	49	32	60.5%	0.2	41	40	50.6%	-5.7
White Sox	2007	38	43	46.9%	-8.2	34	47	42.0%	-3.6
White Sox	2008	55	29	65.5%	17.3	35	48	42.2%	-12
White Sox	2009	43	38	53.1%	-5.2	36	45	44.4%	-2.8
White Sox Total		237	177	57.2%	8	204	209	49.4%	6.8

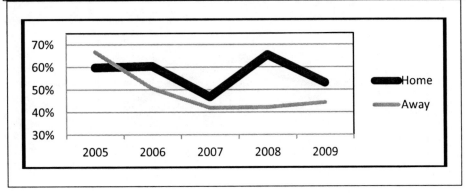

Cincinnati Reds

Team	Year	Hm Win	Hm Loss	Win %	Units	Rd Win	Rd Loss	Win %	Units
Cincinnati	2005	42	39	51.9%	2.2	31	50	38.3%	-9.6
Cincinnati	2006	42	39	51.9%	-4.9	38	43	46.9%	2.3
Cincinnati	2007	39	42	48.1%	-10.4	33	48	40.7%	-5.6
Cincinnati	2008	43	38	53.1%	-3.5	31	50	38.3%	-13.3
Cincinnati	2009	39	41	48.8%	-3.7	39	43	47.6%	8.3
Cincinnati Total		205	199	50.7%	-20.3	172	234	42.4%	-17.9

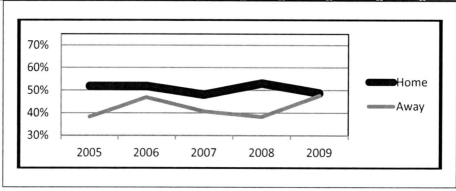

Cleveland Indians

Team	Year	Hm Win	Hm Loss	Win %	Units	Rd Win	Rd Loss	Win %	Units
Cleveland	2005	43	38	53.1%	-12.2	50	31	61.7%	22.6
Cleveland	2006	44	37	54.3%	-3	34	47	42.0%	-12.2
Cleveland	2007	55	30	64.7%	11.4	47	41	53.4%	4.1
Cleveland	2008	45	36	55.6%	-4	36	45	44.4%	-4
Cleveland	2009	35	46	43.2%	-16.3	30	51	37.0%	-15.9
Cleveland Total		222	187	54.3%	-24.1	197	215	47.8%	-5.4

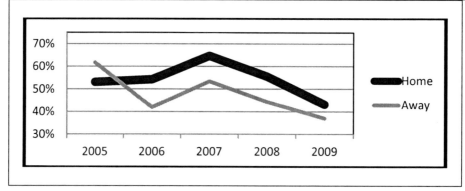

Colorado Rockies

Team	Year	Hm Win	Hm Loss	Win %	Units	Rd Win	Rd Loss	Win %	Units
Colorado	2005	40	41	49.4%	0.3	27	54	33.3%	-11.4
Colorado	2006	44	37	54.3%	2.8	32	49	39.5%	-8.2
Colorado	2007	54	33	62.1%	15.5	43	44	49.4%	11.9
Colorado	2008	43	38	53.1%	-7.4	31	50	38.3%	-13.7
Colorado	2009	51	32	61.4%	7	42	41	50.6%	6.1
Colorado Total		**232**	**181**	**56.2%**	**18.2**	**175**	**238**	**42.4%**	**-15.3**

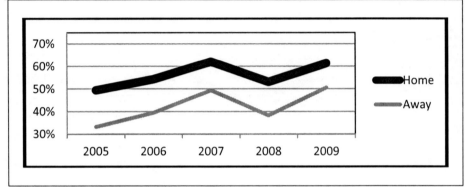

Detroit

Team	Year	Hm Win	Hm Loss	Win %	Units	Rd Win	Rd Loss	Win %	Units
Detroit	2005	39	42	48.1%	-7.9	32	49	39.5%	-11.8
Detroit	2006	51	36	58.6%	-0.9	52	36	59.1%	17.3
Detroit	2007	45	36	55.6%	-4.2	43	38	53.1%	5
Detroit	2008	40	41	49.4%	-18	34	47	42.0%	-12.8
Detroit	2009	51	30	63.0%	10.5	35	47	42.7%	-12.7
Detroit Total		**226**	**185**	**55.0%**	**-20.5**	**196**	**217**	**47.5%**	**-15**

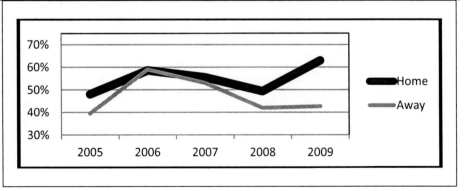

Florida

Team	Year	Hm Win	Hm Loss	Win %	Units	Rd Win	Rd Loss	Win %	Units
Florida	2005	45	36	55.6%	-6.2	38	43	46.9%	-9.2
Florida	2006	42	39	51.9%	1	36	45	44.4%	0.9
Florida	2007	36	45	44.4%	-12.5	35	46	43.2%	0
Florida	2008	45	36	55.6%	10	39	41	48.8%	9.7
Florida	2009	43	38	53.1%	-5.8	44	37	54.3%	14.8
Total		211	194	52.1%	-13.5	192	212	47.5%	16.2

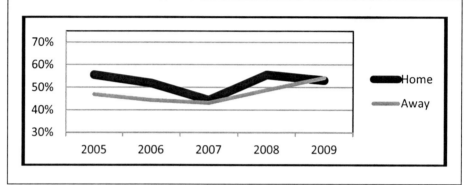

Houston

Team	Year	Hm Win	Hm Loss	Win %	Units	Rd Win	Rd Loss	Win %	Units
Houston	2005	57	31	64.8%	16.8	39	49	44.3%	-8.8
Houston	2006	44	37	54.3%	-7.2	38	43	46.9%	-4.8
Houston	2007	42	39	51.9%	-3.9	31	50	38.3%	-15.1
Houston	2008	47	31	60.3%	13.6	39	44	47.0%	8.1
Houston	2009	44	37	54.3%	3	30	51	37.0%	-12.1
Houston Total		234	175	57.2%	22.3	177	237	42.8%	-32.7

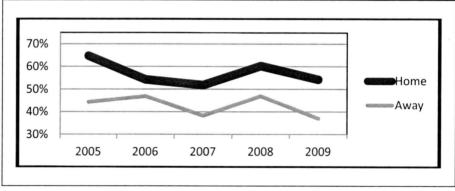

Kansas City

Team	Year	Hm Win	Hm Loss	Win %	Units	Rd Win	Rd Loss	Win %	Unit
KC	2005	34	47	42.0%	1.9	22	59	27.2%	-19.1
KC	2006	34	47	42.0%	3.1	28	53	34.6%	7.8
KC	2007	35	46	43.2%	-7.3	34	47	42.0%	5.2
KC	2008	38	43	46.9%	-6	37	44	45.7%	8.9
KC	2009	33	48	40.7%	-17	32	49	39.5%	-7.4
Kansas City Total		174	231	43.0%	-25.3	153	252	37.8%	-4.6

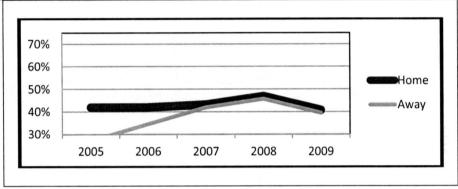

LA Angels

Team	Year	Hm Win	Hm Loss	Win %	Units	Rd Win	Rd Loss	Win %	Units
La Angels	2005	51	36	58.6%	-5.1	48	37	56.5%	14.8
La Angels	2006	45	36	55.6%	-3.1	44	37	54.3%	8
La Angels	2007	54	28	65.9%	10	40	43	48.2%	-6.4
La Angels	2008	50	33	60.2%	0.3	51	32	61.4%	20.3
La Angels	2009	53	33	61.6%	7.5	49	36	57.6%	16.2
La Angels Total		253	166	60.4%	9.6	232	185	55.6%	52.9

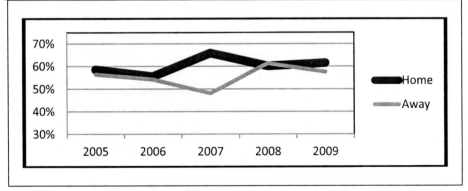

LA Dodgers

Team	Year	Hm Win	Hm Loss	Win %	Units	Rd Win	Rd Loss	Win %	Units
Dodgers	2005	40	41	49.4%	-9.3	31	50	38.3%	-15.7
Dodgers	2006	49	33	59.8%	6.3	39	44	47.0%	-5.7
Dodgers	2007	43	38	53.1%	-4	39	42	48.1%	-2.5
Dodgers	2008	50	35	58.8%	1.8	38	47	44.7%	-11
Dodgers	2009	53	32	62.4%	3.9	46	39	54.1%	3.9
Dodgers Total		235	179	56.8%	-1.3	193	222	46.5%	-31

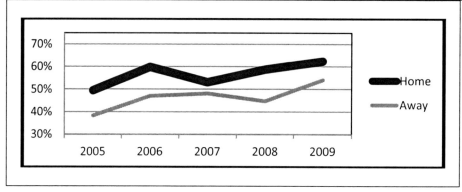

Milwaukee

Team	Year	Hm Win	Hm Loss	Win %	Units	Rd Win	Rd Loss	Win %	Units
Milwaukee	2005	46	35	56.8%	8.3	35	46	43.2%	-3.1
Milwaukee	2006	48	33	59.3%	7.8	27	54	33.3%	-22.8
Milwaukee	2007	51	30	63.0%	11.3	32	49	39.5%	-17.1
Milwaukee	2008	50	33	60.2%	3.5	41	42	49.4%	-0.4
Milwaukee	2009	40	41	49.4%	-11.4	40	41	49.4%	6.6
Milwaukee Total		235	172	57.7%	19.5	175	232	43.0%	-36.8

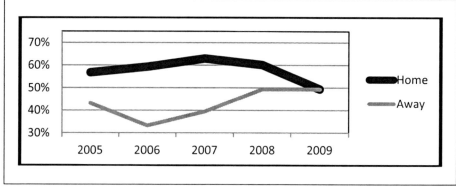

NY Mets

Team	Year	Hm Win	Hm Loss	Win %	Units	Rd Win	Rd Loss	Win %	Units
NY Mets	2005	48	33	59.3%	5.9	35	46	43.2%	-8.6
NY Mets	2006	54	33	62.1%	8.4	49	36	57.6%	9.7
NY Mets	2007	41	40	50.6%	-23.4	47	34	58.0%	11.1
NY Mets	2008	48	33	59.3%	-3.6	41	40	50.6%	-3.3
NY Mets	2009	41	40	50.6%	-1.1	29	52	35.8%	-13.9
NY Mets Total		232	179	56.4%	-13.8	201	208	49.1%	-5

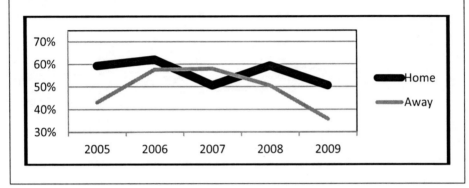

NY Yankees

Team	Year	Hm Win	Hm Loss	Win %	Units	Rd Win	Rd Loss	Win %	Units
Yankees	2005	54	29	65.1%	-2.7	43	41	51.2%	-17.4
Yankees	2006	51	32	61.4%	-10.2	47	36	56.6%	0.6
Yankees	2007	53	30	63.9%	-3.3	42	41	50.6%	-12.2
Yankees	2008	48	33	59.3%	-2.3	41	40	50.6%	-3.7
Yankees	2009	64	25	71.9%	15.3	50	38	56.8%	2.9
Yankees Total		270	149	64.4%	-3.2	223	196	53.2%	-29.8

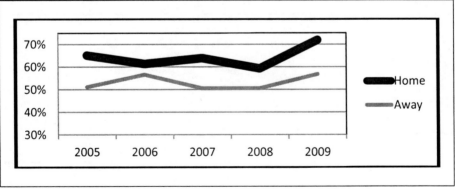

Oakland

Team	Year	Hm Win	Hm Loss	Win %	Units	Rd Win	Rd Loss	Win %	Units
Oakland	2005	45	36	55.6%	-4.6	43	38	53.1%	9.9
Oakland	2006	50	34	59.5%	5.3	46	39	54.1%	13.4
Oakland	2007	40	41	49.4%	-12.2	36	45	44.4%	-3.8
Oakland	2008	42	37	53.2%	-1.5	33	49	40.2%	-6.8
Oakland	2009	40	41	49.4%	-3.4	35	46	43.2%	6.2
Oakland Total		217	189	53.4%	-16.4	193	217	47.1%	18.9

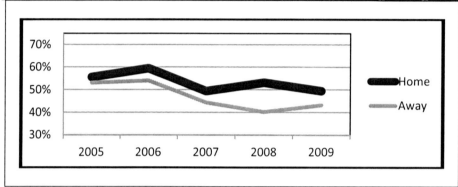

Philadelphia

Team	Year	Hm Win	Hm Loss	Win %	Units	Rd Win	Rd Loss	Win %	Units
Philadelphia	2005	46	35	56.8%	-1.6	42	39	51.9%	4.4
Philadelphia	2006	41	40	50.6%	-13.4	44	37	54.3%	5.6
Philadelphia	2007	47	36	56.6%	2.4	42	40	51.2%	4.3
Philadelphia	2008	55	33	62.5%	5.9	48	40	54.5%	6
Philadelphia	2009	50	39	56.2%	-8.2	52	36	59.1%	12.6
Philadelphia Total		239	183	56.6%	-14.9	228	192	54.3%	32.9

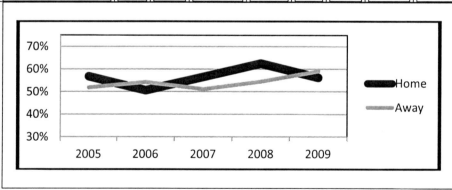

Pittsburgh

Team	Year	Hm Win	Hm Loss	Win %	Units	Rd Win	Rd Loss	Win %	Units
Pittsburgh	2005	34	47	42.0%	-14.5	33	48	40.7%	-1.3
Pittsburgh	2006	43	38	53.1%	9	24	57	29.6%	-21.3
Pittsburgh	2007	37	44	45.7%	-9.1	31	50	38.3%	-7.4
Pittsburgh	2008	39	42	48.1%	-0.9	28	53	34.6%	-11.5
Pittsburgh	2009	40	41	49.4%	2.1	22	58	27.5%	-25.1
Pittsburgh Total		193	212	47.7%	-13.4	138	266	34.2%	66.6

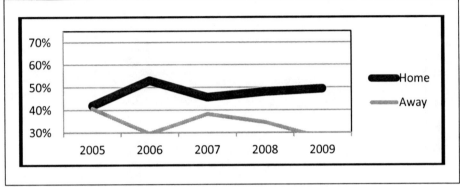

San Diego

Team	Year	Hm Win	Hm Loss	Win %	Units	Rd Win	Rd Loss	Win %	Units
San Diego	2005	46	36	56.1%	-2.1	36	47	43.4%	-8.2
San Diego	2006	43	40	51.8%	-8.3	46	37	55.4%	13.2
San Diego	2007	47	34	58.0%	-1.5	42	40	51.2%	0.6
San Diego	2008	35	46	43.2%	-17.5	28	53	34.6%	-19.7
San Diego	2009	42	39	51.9%	3	33	48	40.7%	0.5
San Diego Total		213	195	52.2%	-26.4	185	225	45.1%	-13.6

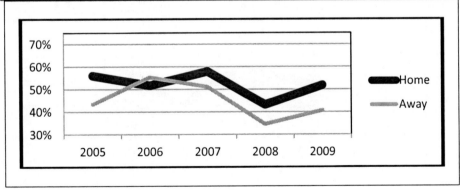

San Francisco

Team	Year	Hm Win	Hm Loss	Win %	Units	Rd Win	Rd Loss	Win %	Units
San Fran	2005	37	44	45.7%	-11.4	38	43	46.9%	4
San Fran	2006	43	38	53.1%	-3.3	33	47	41.3%	-11.8
San Fran	2007	39	42	48.1%	-10.9	32	49	39.5%	-10.1
San Fran	2008	37	44	45.7%	-7.4	35	46	43.2%	2
San Fran	2009	52	29	64.2%	17.4	36	45	44.4%	-4.4
San Fran Total		208	197	51.4%	-15.6	174	230	43.1%	-20.3

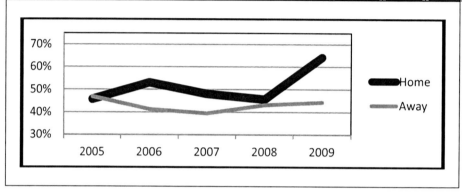

Seattle

Team	Year	Hm Win	Hm Loss	Win %	Units	Rd Win	Rd Loss	Win %	Units
Seattle	2005	39	42	48.1%	-6	30	51	37.0%	-12.5
Seattle	2006	44	37	54.3%	1.6	34	47	42.0%	-6.2
Seattle	2007	49	32	60.5%	13	39	42	48.1%	5.2
Seattle	2008	35	46	43.2%	-14.6	26	55	32.1%	-22.6
Seattle	2009	48	33	59.3%	12.6	37	44	45.7%	0
Seattle Total		215	190	53.1%	6.6	166	239	41.0%	-36.1

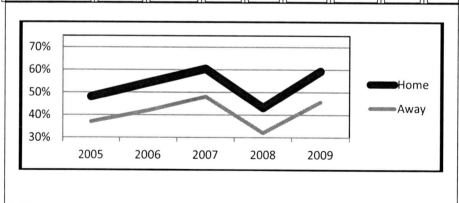

St. Louis

Team	Year	Hm Win	Hm Loss	Win %	Units	Rd Win	Rd Loss	Win %	Units
St Louis	2005	53	33	61.6%	0	52	33	61.2%	9.9
St Louis	2006	55	33	62.5%	4.7	39	50	43.8%	-16.5
St Louis	2007	43	38	53.1%	-1.8	35	46	43.2%	-3.5
St Louis	2008	46	35	56.8%	4.3	40	41	49.4%	5.5
St Louis	2009	46	36	56.1%	-6.7	45	38	54.2%	4.3
St Louis Total		243	175	58.1%	0.5	211	208	50.4%	-0.3

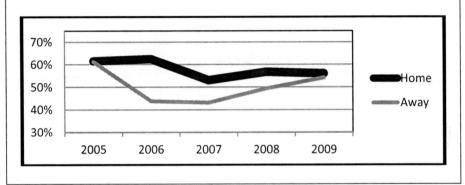

Texas

Team	Year	Hm Win	Hm Loss	Win %	Units	Rd Win	Rd Loss	Win %	Units
Texas	2005	44	37	54.3%	2	35	46	43.2%	-6.9
Texas	2006	39	42	48.1%	-14.5	41	40	50.6%	7.5
Texas	2007	47	34	58.0%	13.7	28	53	34.6%	-10.9
Texas	2008	40	41	49.4%	-3.2	39	42	48.1%	9.9
Texas	2009	48	33	59.3%	7.9	39	42	48.1%	4.7
Total		218	187	53.8%	5.9	182	223	44.9%	4.3

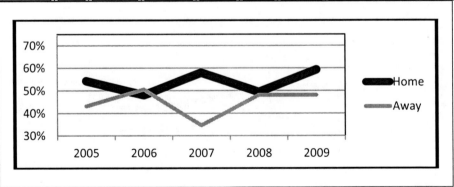

Toronto

Team	Year	Hm Win	Hm Loss	Win %	Units	Rd Win	Rd Loss	Win %	Units
Toronto	2005	43	38	53.1%	3.4	37	44	45.7%	5.3
Toronto	2006	50	31	61.7%	10	37	44	45.7%	-9.7
Toronto	2007	49	32	60.5%	10	34	47	42.0%	-9.7
Toronto	2008	47	34	58.0%	1.8	39	42	48.1%	-0.1
Toronto	2009	44	37	54.3%	-0.9	31	50	38.3%	-13.9
Toronto Total		233	172	57.5%	24.3	178	227	44.0%	-28.1

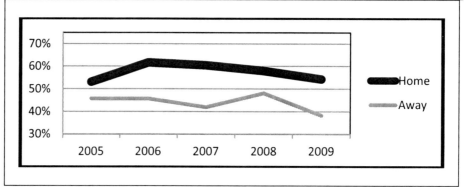

Washington

Team	Year	Hm Win	Hm Loss	Win %	Units	Rd Win	Rd Loss	Win %	Units
Wash	2005	41	40	50.6%	-6.5	40	41	49.4%	13.4
Wash	2006	41	40	50.6%	1.8	30	51	37.0%	-8.3
Wash	2007	40	41	49.4%	8.5	33	48	40.7%	6.7
Wash	2008	34	46	42.5%	-9.1	25	56	30.9%	-15.5
Wash	2009	33	48	40.7%	-12.3	26	55	32.1%	-14.1
Wash Total		189	215	46.8%	-17.6	154	251	38.0%	-17.8

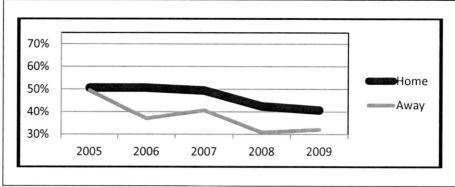

GETAWAY DAYS AND OTHER SYSTEMS

A system that has popped up in recent years has been playing unders on getaway day. Getaway day is always a mess for teams. A visiting team (and home team at times) finishes up a series and heads off to the next city. Typically played during the day, teams want to get in as early as possible to be ready for the next day's game. It isn't easy. Up to seven thousand pounds of equipment has be packed, loaded, and moved onto that night's flight.

But teams have it simple compared to umpires. Umpires don't have a squad of equipment managers loading their gear. They don't have chartered flights waiting at the airport for the team to arrive. Umpires fly commercial. They have flight reservations, and they don't like to miss them.

And so the theory of playing unders on get-away days sounds like it has some legs to it. Teams aren't in the mood to lengthen a game. Umpires certainly are going to move things along, even stretching the strike zone out to hurry things up. Star players might get the day game off after playing the night before. Small crowds make many stadiums seem like a morgue in these mid-week afternoon games. Add all these factors up and you have a game that screams out "UNDER!"

But do the facts support this theory? In recent years, the answer is a resounding yes. In 2008, a $100 bettor blindly playing unders in get-away games would have made $7,590 (+6.3% ROI). Last year, unders in getaway situations earned +4.3 ROI, a total profit of $5,250 net profit for a $100 bettor.

This is just a short two-year trend, however. In 2007, the ROI for getaway day was -2.7% ROI. The year before, it was -6.4% ROI. In 2005, -2.3% ROI. 2004? -2.2% ROI. Maybe that get-away day theory doesn't hold much water.

Angles always make a little bit of sense. The trick is to know that many other factors come into play besides angles and to verify these situations with your own research. The data is out there; a bettor just has to put in the work. Below are twelve other angles used by baseball bettors. Some have worked in the past; some haven't. Who's to say that they will work in 2010?

A bettor shouldn't ignore systems, but it is important that he keeps them in proper context. The game is still pitcher vs. batter, and any single individual can make a system worthless.

Trend #1: Play on any team that committed four or more errors in its previous game.

Reason: Teams that aren't focused on a game make more mistakes. After making numerous errors and embarrassing itself, a team will be highly focused in its next game.

Verdict: It depends on the location of the next game. Home teams are 52-27 in games immediately after committing four or more errors. Home favorites are 37-13 for +17.5 units (21.6% Return on investment). Home dogs are 15-14 for +5.5 units (18.5% ROI).

However, road teams are just 30-49 after committing four or more errors in a game. Road favorites are 10-12 for -6.3 units (-20% ROI). Road dogs are 20-37 for -11 units (-19% ROI).

Trend #2: Play on any team that scored more than 10 runs in its previous game.

Reason: A team that scored 10 runs in its last game is playing at its peak and is underpriced at this time.

Verdict: Home favorites rock in these situations, going 370-215 for a return on investment of 3.7%. Home dogs break even (94-114 straight up record). Road teams aren't so fortunate. Road dogs have a 191-285 record for a ROI of -5.1%. Road favorites were 155-125 for a ROI of -4.3%

All in all, this angle is worthless.

System #3: Fade starters pitching on three day's rest.

Reason: Pitchers have developed their arms to have at least four days of recovery before making their next start. Cutting that recovery time down by one day means the pitcher is not throwing at full strength and is overvalued.

Verdict: Mixed. Overall, starters going on three day's rest are 106-106 (0% ROI). However, road teams facing short-rest starters are 48-55 for +2.4% ROI. Breaking it down even further, road favorites in this situation are 14-7 for

+17.7% ROI. Road dogs are just 31-48 for -7% ROI. Home teams are 60-53 with a slight loss (-2.5% ROI). Overall, there isn't much value fading short-rest starters blindly. That isn't to say on a case by case basis this is true. Some pitchers can likely handle these situations, others can't.

System #4: Play on any team that has scored in at least five individual innings in their previous game.

Reason: "You can never go wrong when you bet on a hot team."

Verdict: There is nothing to this prospective system. Teams in this situation are 141-135 for -4 units, a ROI of -.5%. It is coin flipping at its finest.

System #5: Play on any home team coming off a road trip.

Reason: Playing in front of friendly fans and a familiar field will help a team relax and focus on the game. No going through the motions here.

Verdict: It depends. Home dogs were 280-321 in these situations, good for a +3.5% ROI. Home favorites were 846-620 for -3.2% ROI. Focus on home dogs and you should do OK.

System #6: Play on any home team that got shut out in its previous game at home.

Reason: Teams that have been embarrassed in front of their home crowd will be much more focused the next time out.

Verdict: Home teams that got shut out in its last game were 371-325, good for -18 units overall. Home dogs were at the break-even point (104-127 overall), but home favorites got crushed (-2.2% ROI).

System #7: Play on any rested home team who is playing an unrested opponent.

Reason: Road teams that played the day before will lack focus compared to its well-rested opponents who are playing at home.

Verdict: Home dogs dominate in these situations, going 76-72 for +13.5% ROI. Home favorites aren't as solid, breaking even over the course of 300 games.

System #8: Play on any home team in the Eastern Time Zone playing a team whose previous game was in the Pacific Time Zone

Reason: It is tough for a team to play at its peak if that team has to travel cross country, losing three hours of clock time in the process.

Verdict: Home teams were 192-154 in these situations, good for a +8% ROI.

System #9: Play any underdog in a division game

Reason: Teams are much more focused since division games have more meaning than non-divisional games. They also have better awareness of the opponent's weaknesses, leveling the differences in skill.

Verdict: This system won't make a bettor rich, but it does show an overall profit. Since the start of tracking, underdogs in these situations are 2751-3570, good for a ROI of +1.9%.

System #10: Play on any home team in the cold weather (under 60 degrees) facing an opponent coming off a warm weather game (over 75 degrees)

Reason: It will typically take a team some time to adjust to bad weather, especially if the team had been playing in good weather.

Verdict: The situations don't come up often, but home dogs are extremely live in these instances. In 17 games, the home team was 11-6 for +760, good for a ROI of 45%. Caution: small sample size alert.

System #11: Play on any home dogs when the crowd is expected to be above 35,000.

Reason: It is easier to fight against the odds when the crowd is pushing you along.

Verdict: This system shows some profit with a ROI of 2.9% over 1400 games wagered. The straight up record for home dogs in these situations is 681-783.

System #12: Play on any home dog when the crowd is expected to be below 12,000

Reason: Just as it is easy for home dogs to get up for a game with a big crowd, it is equally difficult for away favorites to get up for a game with a small crowd.

Verdict: Home dogs have a 136-147 record in games where the crowd is below 12,000, good for a ROI of 8.3%.

You can use all the quantitative data you can get, but you still have to distrust it and use your own intelligence and judgment.

Alvin Toffler

The only thing that one really knows about human nature is that it changes. Change is the one quality we can predicate of it. The systems that fail are those that rely on the permanency of human nature, and not on its growth and development. The error of Louis XIV was that he thought human nature would always be the same. The result of his error was the French Revolution. It was an admirable result.

Oscar Wilde

MEASURING OFFENSE

"There is no clock in baseball". One often hears this particular argument in debates over the 'quality' of a sport. This argument concerning baseball may be true in a technical sense. You obviously have seen the average time of a nine inning game go up over the years. But it is false in an n abstract sense of the word.

In baseball, the ticking clock doesn't measure time. It measures something far more scarce than minutes or seconds in a football game. The baseball clock measures outs. A team has three outs for an inning and 27 for a game. Its offensive abilities are measured against the backdrop of this ticking clock. If a batter gets on base, he succeeds. If he generates an out, he fails.

A team scores runs by putting batters on base and driving them in. The art needed in rating pitching is not required to judge offensive power: offense is for the most part simply math.

It is here we get into the nuts and bolts of measuring a team's offense. Getting on base is measured by on-base percentage. A bettor takes all the times a team gets on base, and divides that by how many times they are at bat. The linear equation is:

OB percentage = (Hits plus Walks plus Hit by Pitch) divided by (At bats plus Hit by Pitch plus Sac Flies).

The average on-base percentage for teams is around .336, with American League teams usually higher due to the designated hitter rule. The extremes are sometimes severe: Yankees' on-base percentage was .362 while the Mariners had an on-base percentage of just .314.

On base percentage tells us how often a team gets on base. However, an offense still must have the ability to drive that runner home. Slugging percentage is the best tool available to show us how well a team can do this. The equation for slugging percentage is:

SLG percentage = (Hits plus Doubles plus (Triples multiplied by 2) plus (Homers multiplied by 3)) divided by at-bats.

In 2009, the AL slugged .428 and the NL slugged .409.

To translate these two numbers into an understandable offensive power rating, I simply multiply a team's on-base percentage with its slugging percentage. This number (call it OTS) means nothing by itself. However, if I divide the team OTS by the league average OTS, I get something I can work with. Boston slugged .454 with a .352 on base percentage. Its raw OTS number, .160, divided by the league average OTS (.336*.420=.144) equals 111%. Boston's offense is 11% above league average. The table below shows each American League team's OTS power number along with its runs scored power rating:

Team	OTS	OTS/LG	RPG/LG
Orioles	.138	96%	95%
Red Sox	.160	111%	112%
White Sox	.135	94%	93%
Indians	.141	98%	99%
Tigers	.138	96%	95%
Royals	.129	90%	88%
Angels	.154	107%	113%
Twins	.148	103%	104%
Yankees	.173	120%	117%
A's	.130	91%	97%
Mariners	.126	88%	82%
Rays	.151	105%	103%
Rangers	.142	99%	100%
Blue Jays	.147	102%	102%
League	**.144**		

There are a few other offensive formulas developed in recent years that are slightly more accurate than the standard OTS formulas. Bill James, Clay Davenport, Keith Woolner, Phil Birnbaum, and Neil Bonner in particular deserve special mention for creating new statistics that measure a player's offensive contribution. Part of the problem with these formulas, however, is the degree of difficulty involved in the stat. The increased effort isn't worth the increase in accuracy.

The common availability of OTS also plays a large role in why I like the stat. Every website worth its salt has on base percentage and slugging percentage readily available. ESPN.com, yahoo.com, mlb.com and others also break these numbers down into different splits. When handicapping a team's offensive abilities, I look deeper than just raw OTS numbers. I want to know that team's OTS numbers on the road, at home, against righties, lefties, last twenty games, last fifty games, and so on.

By sticking with OTS, I am able to measure those factors. I can also determine if a team is getting "fluky" runs or not scoring at the rate its statistics would indicate. Seattle is one good example. Its OTS rating was 88%. Its actual run production was 82%, a significant difference.

A little investigation shows that the Mariners batted .234 with runners in scoring position compared to its overall average of .258. Clutch hitting, or lack of clutch hitting, is not a repeatable skill. Seattle's offensive performance will likely improve. I'll be able to adjust the Mariners' offensive power rating upward thanks to knowing how they have performed in the clutch. It is difficult to do that with other, more complicated, formulas.

EXPLOITING DEFENSE

When a surprise team busts out of the gates early in the season, one key factor could be the team's defense. Offense is usually predictable and easy to forecast. A team averaging six runs a game is going to do pretty well. Not so with pitching. A pitcher with a 1.30 ERA may be good, lucky, or have a great defense behind him.

In baseball, what we often think is good pitching may simply be good defense. An elite pitcher like Tim Lincecum can create his own outs by striking out batters. Lower class pitchers like Jon Garland and Zach Duke are forced to use their defense to get outs, leaving these types of pitchers vulnerable to poor defense.

The quickest way to measure the quality of a team's defense is the Defensive Efficiency Ratio developed by Bill James. DER is a formula that calculates how often a ball hit into the field of play is turned into an out:

1 - ((Hits Allowed - Home Runs Allowed) divided by (At Bats - Strikeouts - Home Runs))

The average rate for a team is usually around 69%. In other words, a ball hit into the field of play typically will be turned into an out 69% of the time. Teams with a higher number typically help its pitching staff; a rate under 69% means a pitcher is getting hurt by his defense.

The best defense in the major leagues last year was the Los Angeles Dodgers. LA's defense turned 71.1% of its opportunities into outs. Less base runners, less runs scored. Seattle was the best defensive team in the American League, quite a turnaround from a 2008 season that saw the Mariners finish second from the bottom in DER. The table below shows how each team performed with the gloves in 2009.

Team	R/G	DER	Team	R/G	DER
LAD	3.77	.711	SEA	4.27	.710
SFG	3.77	.704	NYY	4.65	.695
CIN	4.46	.702	TEX	4.57	.695
CHC	4.17	.695	TBR	4.65	.693
STL	3.95	.692	DET	4.57	.692
NYM	4.67	.691	CHW	4.52	.687
PHI	4.75	.691	MIN	4.69	.687
SDP	4.77	.690	LAA	4.70	.685
PIT	5.05	.689	OAK	4.70	.680
MIL	4.41	.688	TOR	4.76	.680
COL	3.96	.686	BAL	5.41	.678
ATL	4.73	.685	CLE	5.34	.678
FLA	4.83	.684	BOS	4.54	.677
ARI	5.40	.680	KCR	5.20	.673
WSN	4.75	.680			
HOU	4.63	.676			
LEAGUE		.690	LEAGUE	4.75	.686

As a crude but passable rule of thumb, each 1% difference in team DER is worth five cents to a bettor. It is just a rule of thumb. The defensive ability of a team can change drastically from season to season, week to week, and game to game. As injuries take their toll, and players get days off or shipped out, the defense quality of a team can fluctuate greatly.

One also has to take park factors into account as well. Boston's DER will typically be lower than its actual performance thanks to the small foul grounds and Green Monster in Fenway. Keeping track of these fluctuations can be an important tool in predicting which pitching staffs get on a roll, and which ones will struggle due to conditions outside its control. One last warning: the quality of pitching has some impact on a team's DER. It isn't a huge impact, but a noticeable one. The DER method isn't perfect but it does help evaluate a team.

THE PITCHER'S TOOLBOX

A handicapper can use a wide range of tools to determine the expected performance level of a starting pitcher. None tells the whole story but each adds a piece to the puzzle we are constantly trying to solve. Some of these include:

EARNED RUN AVERAGE

The most common statistic is the Earned Run Average (ERA). The ERA is the number of earned runs a pitcher allows per nine innings on the mound. To determine a pitcher's ERA, you multiply the total earned runs by nine then divides that total by the number of innings pitched. The American League ERA in 2009 was 4.68; in the National League, it was 4.63. Scoring in both leagues increased from the 2008 season, where the NL ERA was 4.29 ERA and the AL's ERA was 4.35.

The ERA has too many flaws to be useful as a handicapping tool. The most obvious one is its failure to account for a starter's relief pitching. If a pitcher is pulled from the game with the bases loaded and one out, that pitcher may not get charged with an earned run if the relief pitcher does his job. If the reliever melts down, the starter gets charged with all three runs. Both circumstances were out of the starter's control, but its impact on his ERA is awfully strong.

It isn't worthless, however. The ERA is used by everyone as a quick reference to a pitcher's quality. If someone says a pitcher's ERA is 2.00, I know immediately that the pitcher is probably pretty good. That serves a good purpose. I often use a pitcher's ERA to illustrate a point, but many more other tools are available to show a pitcher's skill.

EXPECTED ERA (xERA)

xERA is a tool used to take some of the "noise" away from a pitcher's earned run average. A pitcher's xERA isn't affected by his bullpen support or defense. The formula for xERA is:

Step 1		.575 * Hits Allowed Per Nine Innings
Step 2	Plus	.94 * Home Runs Allowed Per Nine
Step 3	Plus	.28 * Walks Allowed Per Nine
Step 4	Minus	.01 * Strikeouts Per Nine
Step 5	Minus	2.68

Usually xERA is in the same neighborhood as a pitcher's true ERA. When there is a difference in the two numbers, however, a bettor should be prepared to dig deeper into the pitcher's performance. Differences less than half a run can be discounted; differences greater than .50 indicates a possibility of betting on or against the pitcher. When given a choice between ERA and xERA, choose xERA. This number is more accurate regarding future performance than a pitcher's true ERA.

If a pitcher's xERA is higher than his actual ERA, then he got a bit lucky. His ERA will likely rise. If his xERA is lower than his ERA, then the pitcher threw better than the numbers indicate. He is a good pick to be undervalued when the line is made.

FIELDING INDEPENDENT PITCHING (FIP) ERA

Similar to the above formula, FIP ERA was designed to measure only the variables that the pitcher has completely controls. Tangotiger, co-author of The Book and new employee of the Seattle Mariners, developed this formula. It assumes pitchers have control over only home runs, strikeouts, and walks. Everything else, base hits, errors, runs...all those can be chalked up to random chance. As The Hardball Times said, FIP ERA tells you how well the pitcher pitched, regardless of how well his fielders fielded.

One negative to FIP ERA is the heavy influence home runs have on the number. A pitcher's home run rate varies from year to year so one must be careful when to apply this.

FIP ERA= ((HR*13) + ((BB+HBP)*3) – (K's *2) / Innings pitched) +3.20

Step 1		Home Runs *13
Step 2	Plus	(Walks Plus Hit Batters) *3
Step 3	Minus	Strikeouts * 2
Step 4	Divided by	Innings Pitched
Step 5	Plus	3.2

FIP can also be tweaked by replacing the pitcher's home run rate to the league average home run per fly ball rate. This adjustment, called xFIP, tends to be a better predictor of a pitcher's future performance. If you have to choose one and only one statistic to forecast a pitcher's future, xFIP is it.

DEFENSE INDEPENDENT PITCHING STATS (DIPS) ERA

Voros McCracken created this groundbreaking statistic. It is an extremely complicated formula, designed by McCracken to show that pitchers have far less impact on turning batted balls into outs than previously thought. The reasoning behind McCracken's work can be a valuable tool to handicapping, but the DIPS ERA may be too complicated to be of much direct use in handicapping.

POWER/FINESSE RATING

This formula is used to determine how reliant a pitcher is on his defense. It measures how often a pitcher allows balls to be hit into the field of play. Finesse pitchers need a good defense behind them to succeed. Power pitchers can get away with having a bad defense. The formula is:

> (WALKS PLUS STRIKEOUTS) DIVIDED BY INNINGS PITCHED

A rating above 1.10 denotes a power pitcher. The twenty starting pitchers with the highest Power/Finesse rating are listed below:

Player	P/F Rate		Player	Age
Harden, Rich	1.7		Parra, Manny	1.4
Sanchez, Jonathan	1.6		Masterson, Justin	1.4
Kershaw, Clayton	1.6		Scherzer, Max	1.4
Gallardo, Yovani	1.6		Verlander, Justin	1.4
de la Rosa, Jorge	1.5		Liriano, Francisco	1.4
Lincecum, Tim	1.5		Zambrano, Carlos	1.4
Gaudin, Chad	1.5		Billingsley, Chad	1.3
Lester, Jon	1.4		Garza, Matt	1.3
Burnett, A.J.	1.4		Chamberlain, Joba	1.3

The sixteen starting pitchers with the lowest Power/Finesse rating in 2008: These pitchers are vulnerable to poor defense.

Player	P/F Rate		Player	Age
Pineiro, Joel	0.6		Sowers, Jeremy	0.8
Stammen, Craig	0.7		Huff, David	0.8
Blackburn, Nick	0.7		Garland, Jon	0.8

Buehrle, Mark	0.7		Looper, Braden	0.8
Duke, Zach	0.7		Washburn, Jarrod	0.8
Geer, Josh	0.7		Moyer, Jamie	0.8
Lannan, John	0.8		Guthrie, Jeremy	0.9
Bergesen, Brad	0.8		Hunter, Tommy	0.9
Cook, Aaron	0.8		Arroyo, Bronson	0.9

Other pitching tools that help a bettor determine the talent level of a pitcher:

WALKS/HITS RATIO (WHIP)

The formula is simple: add the walks and hits together, and divide by innings pitched. Look on WHIP as a form of a pitcher's On Base Percentage. It is very useful when combined with other statistics, but can cause mistakes if a bettor focuses primarily on this stat. Ground ball pitchers typically have higher WHIPs than fly ball pitchers.

GROUND BALL PITCHERS

Taken as a group, ground ball pitchers give up more hits and strike out fewer batters than fly ball pitchers. That doesn't mean they are less effective, however. While ground ball pitchers allow more base runners than the typical fly ball pitcher, they also give up fewer home runs. The best way to determine a pitcher's ground ball tendencies is obviously his ground ball rate. 42% is league average. Anything above 50% is good, while anything below 35% means the pitcher is prone to giving up an ill-time home run. The chart below lists the most extreme ground ball pitchers in 2009 and their home run rates per nine innings.

Player	HR/9	G%		Player	HR/9	G%
Pineiro, Joel	0.5	60		Lannan, John	1.0	52
Cook, Aaron	1.1	57		Maholm, Paul	0.6	52
Lowe, Derek	0.7	56		Anderson, Brett	1.0	51
Marquis, Jason	0.6	56		Hampton, Mike	1.0	51
Carmona, Fausto	1.1	55		Pelfrey, Mike	0.9	51
Carpenter, Chris	0.3	55		Palmer, Matt	0.9	51
Porcello, Rick	1.2	54		Wainwright, Adam	0.7	51
Romero, Ricky	0.9	54		Bannister, Brian	0.9	50

Masterson, Justin	0.8	54		Halladay, Roy	0.8	50
Hernandez, Felix	0.6	53		Bergesen, Brad	0.8	50
Jimenez, Ubaldo	0.5	53		Johnson, Josh	0.6	50
Lannan, John	1.0	52		Volstad, Chris	1.6	49

FLY BALL PITCHERS

Fly ball pitchers are far more affected by weather and ballpark than ground ball pitchers; you certainly don't want to bet on Chris Young when the wind is blowing out to center field in Wrigley Park. But at home in San Diego, Chris Young is a very effective pitcher. Those fly balls that might land in the seats at Wrigley are caught on the warning track at Petco Field. Generally speaking, fly ball pitchers are prone to struggle unless the pitcher has the ability to create strikeouts. Keep an eye out for pitchers with a fly ball rate over 40% if they can't get strikeouts. The chart below lists the most extreme fly-ball pitchers and their home run rates:

Player	HR/9	F%		Player	HR/9	F%
Hernandez, David	2.4	53		Bush, David	1.5	45
Lilly, Ted	1.1	51		Harden, Rich	1.5	44
Weaver, Jered	1.1	50		Sanchez, Jonathan	1.0	43
Redding, Tim	1.4	48		Garza, Matt	1.1	43
Santana, Johan	1.1	48		Washburn, Jarrod	1.2	43
Kazmir, Scott	1.0	48		Happ, J.A.	1.1	43
Wakefield, Tim	0.8	47		Sowers, Jeremy	0.8	43
Guthrie, Jeremy	1.6	47		Tallet, Brian	1.1	43
Baker, Scott S	1.3	47		Verlander, Justin	0.8	43
Karstens, Jeff	1.0	46		Braden, Dallas	0.6	43
Richmond, Scott	1.8	45		Ohlendorf, Ross	1.3	42

COMMAND RATE

The command rate is strikeouts divided by walks. Ideally, you want pitchers to have a 2.0 rate or more. These pitchers, even when struggling, will likely show a sharp rate of improvement over the short and long term. If a pitcher has a control rate under 1.0, he is treading dangerous waters.

The command rate is not perfect; it weighs strikeouts and walks equally and tends to overvalue junk ballers (see Joel Pineiro) who give up a ton of hits but walk few batters. A pitcher that walks two and strikes out seven is more impressive than a pitcher that walks only one and strikes out four. The command rate says differently, but this is a case where common sense should overrule an otherwise solid statistic. Once a bettor accounts for these exceptions, the command rate is an extremely effective tool.

Player	Cmd		Player	Cmd
Haren, Dan	5.9		Pavano, Carl	3.8
Halladay, Roy	5.9		Beckett, Josh	3.6
Vazquez, Javier	5.4		Kuroda, Hiroki	3.6
Greinke, Zack Z	4.7		Lester, Jon T	3.5
Nolasco, Ricky	4.4		Baker, Scott S	3.4
Verlander, Justin B	4.3		Johnson, Josh	3.3
Lilly, Ted	4.2		Harang, Aaron	3.3
Lee, Cliff	4.2		Anderson, Brett	3.3
Hamels, Cole M	3.9		Oswalt, Roy	3.3
Pineiro, Joel	3.9		Peavy, Jake	3.2
Lincecum, Tim	3.8		Wainwright, Adam	3.2
Carpenter, Chris	3.8		Santana, Johan	3.2

DOMINANCE

There is a school of thought in baseball that a strikeout is just another out. A batter whose 300 outs in a season include 180 strikeouts does not hurt his team any more than a batter who strikes out 40 times while making the same 300 outs. I don't buy this argument. When a batter makes contact with a pitch, anything can happen. When a batter strikes out, nothing happens but a slow trip back to the dugout (the Angels and A.J. Pierzneski may disagree with that, however).

Strikeouts show how well a pitcher can dominate a game. About 70% of all batted balls fall in for base hits. Strikeouts eliminate this possibility, and allow a pitcher to escape the errors, bloop hits and broken bat singles that typically plague pitchers.

A pitcher's ability to create outs on his own is called Dominance. The formula for dominance is strikeouts divided by innings pitched multiplied by nine.

Roger Clemens had 218 strikeouts in 214 regular season innings in 2005. His Dominance rate works out to be 218 / 214 * 9 = 9.16. In 2009, Javier Vazquez struck out 238 batters in 219 innings; his Dom rate was 9.8. The most dominant pitchers will have Dom rates over eight while the least dominant will have a rate under five. The typical American League starter will have a Dominance rate around 6.5. The National League, where the pitcher bats, has an average is around 6.8.

One flaw in this statistic is its failure to account for the number of batters faced by a pitcher in an inning. In 2009, Jonathon Sanchez struck out 177 batters in 163 innings, good for a Dominance rate of 9.8. He also walked 88 batters. All told, Sanchez struck out 24.8% of the hitters he faced in 2009. Vazquez, with the same Dom rate as Sanchez, struck out 27% of batters faced. Pitchers who face a lot of hitters have a better chance of racking up a higher Dominance rating. To adjust for this, one should look at a pitchers command rate to see if it confirms his dominance rate.

Player	K9		Player	K9
Harden, Rich	10.9		Scherzer, Max	9.2
Lincecum, Tim	10.4		Haren, Dan	8.8
Verlander, Justin B	10.1		Burnett, A.J.	8.5
Lester, Jon T	10.1		Gaudin, Chad	8.5
Gallardo, Yovani	9.9		Beckett, Josh	8.4
Vazquez, Javier	9.8		Rodriguez, Wandy	8.4
Sanchez, Jonathan O	9.8		Garza, Matt	8.4
Kershaw, Clayton	9.7		Masterson, Justin	8.3
Peavy, Jake	9.7		Hernandez, Felix A	8.2
Greinke, Zack Z	9.5		Wainwright, Adam	8.2
Nolasco, Ricky	9.5		Jimenez, Ubaldo	8.2
de la Rosa, Jorge A	9.4		Johnson, Josh	8.2

CONTROL RATE

The control rate is walks divided by innings pitched multiplied by nine. This number will show you the pitcher's ability to throw the ball over the plate.

You are looking for pitchers that have a control rate less than 2.7. A starter with the ability to strikeout batters will usually be able to overcome a bad control rate

Player	BB9		Player	BB9
Snell, Ian	5.2		Harden, Rich	4.3
Carmona, Fausto C	5.0		Liriano, Francisco	4.3
Parra, Manny	5.0		Laffey, Aaron	4.2
Kershaw, Clayton	4.8		Burnett, A.J.	4.2
Owings, Micah B	4.8		Richard, Clayton	4.2
Davies, Kyle	4.8		Wellemeyer, Todd	4.2
Sanchez, Jonathan O	4.8		Galarraga, Armando	4.2
Davis, Doug	4.6		Masterson, Justin	4.2
Gallardo, Yovani	4.6		Palmer, Matt	4.1
Gaudin, Chad	4.6		Zambrano, Carlos	4.1
Chamberlain, Joba	4.3		Hernandez, David	4.1

PITCHING INJURIES

It isn't easy finding out about injuries. Players often hide them, worried about being Wally Pipp-ed out of the lineup. New HIPAA laws restrict the amount of information that can be released to the media. Teams order their doctors and trainers to keep away from the media, further limiting the amount of information available to fans and the media. Bettors often have to read between the lines and speculate to determine how an injury is affecting a player.

There are some rules of thumbs to use when concerned about injuries. The first is to make sure you know a pitcher's injury history. Staying healthy is a skill. If a pitcher has had a series of injuries over the years, chances are he suddenly isn't going to find perfect health. Keep a sharper eye on these types of pitchers. A pitcher who has been injured the year before will be more likely to get hurt the previous year.

Another concern for bettors is the possibility of a pitcher hiding an injury. Daisuke Matsuzaka admitted this past off-season that he injured his leg in spring training, causing him to change his mechanics and contributed to his shoulder problems in 2009. "I didn't want them to think I was making excuses," he explained. Injuries are a sign of weakness in most players' minds. They'll fight through them as much as possible.

Causes of arm injuries for pitchers

There are four major catalysts for a pitcher getting hurt:

- Bad mechanics: if your throwing technique is poor, the likelihood of an injury is much higher. Guys like Chris Carpenter, Mark Prior, Kerry Wood and BJ Ryan can be effective, but the risk of injury is always higher due to the way they throw the ball. CC Sabathia and Cliff Lee have superb mechanics and should continue to be workhorses in the future.

- Poor conditioning: a pitcher uses his whole body when throwing the ball at top velocity. It isn't the arm that needs to be built up. A pitcher's upper legs and lower torso are the most important part of his throwing motion. If these lack strength and flexibility, problems may arise.

- Overload: when a pitcher throws too many pitches in one game.

- Overuse: when a pitcher throws too often and doesn't have enough time between starts to properly recover.

How to detect arm problems:

- The pitcher starts taking more time between pitches on the mound.
- The pitcher's arm slot is "lower" than normal.
- The pitcher flinches when he releases a pitch.
- The pitcher skips out on his throwing sessions between starts.
- The pitcher doesn't extend his arm all the way on his follow through.
- The pitcher won't throw all the pitches in his arsenal.
- The pitcher "rushes his motion", trying to get more power with his pitches.

Teams are aware that few players are at 100% every day of the season, especially pitchers. A sore arm is not a surprise, and most pitchers are expected to work through it. A 90% Tim Lincecum is still far better than long reliever waiting to make a spot start. The key is to find out when Lincecum is only 90%.

DEALING WITH BULLPENS

Bullpens can be called the Russian roulette of baseball. A handicapper can reasonably estimate how well a team will hit, and how well the starting pitcher will throw. But not so much with the bullpen. A bettor doesn't know who will be pitching, when he will be pitching, or who that pitcher will be throwing against.

It isn't just bettors who have problems. Managers are hired and fired based on their abilities to handle the bullpen. Opinions vary widely on just how to use a closer, middle reliever, left-handed specialist, and so on. Simply put: it is tricky for both experts in the game and bettors to predict what the bullpen performance will be from game to game.

On top of that, the randomness of relief pitching makes it difficult to trust the numbers put up by a bullpen. A pitcher doesn't throw enough innings to make the numbers very credible. But that is what we are left with, so we have to make the best of it.

There are three numbers that I start off with to determine the overall strength of a bullpen:

- Cumulative ERA: This is simply the ERA of the team's bullpen. Everything counts, from the first inning numbers when a starter gets knocked out to the extra inning game.
- ERA from the 7th inning on: This stat counts starters who go deep into the game. It eliminates the innings where a starting pitcher gets knocked out early and the long reliever throws.
- Late and close: tells me how strong the key members of the bullpen are. The typical pitchers in these games are the main setup man and the closer.

The main reason I use these three numbers is that they are available on various websites and are simple to download into a spreadsheet. These are just the base rates I use to start estimating my bullpen power numbers for a particular game, however. More work needs to be done.

Each team generally carries seven relief pitchers: One closer, a couple of set-up men, one or two left-handed specialists, and one or two long relievers/emergency starter types. When Carlos Zambrano is on the mound, you can automatically discard all but two relievers. If Zambrano gets roughed up, chances are the bet is lost regardless of how well the long relievers pitch. Since he will usually go deep into a game and hand the ball over with the lead, I will only care about which relievers finish the 8th and 9th innings. In his case, I'll give much more weight to the "Late and Close" ERA of a team.

If Carlos Silva is starting for the Cubs instead of Zambrano, I will lower the bullpen rating a significant amount. Silva won't go deep into games and will force the middle relievers to carry some of the load in the game. Rather than having Carlos Marmol close out the game, we are forced to hope the back end of the pen can keep the Cubs in the ball game. For that reason, I may put more emphasis on the overall rating of a bullpen rather than focus on the "late and close" numbers.

One also has to take into account how well rested a team's bullpen is. If a closer has thrown three straight days, he won't be on the mound that day. If the setup man went two innings the day before, he may only be available for one inning. Daily charts regarding bullpen use are a must. A team's power rating for the bullpen can swing up or down dramatically depending on who is available.

There are no simple ways to judge a bullpen. A bettor has to be flexible, pay close attention to the use of a team's pitchers, and hope for the best. If done correctly, a bettor will find proper bullpen ratings to be one of the more profitable angles in baseball.

Relief pitchers can handle a much heavier workload than current managers are imposing. Over a five-day period, when relief pitchers are given 16 to 24 batters, their performance is unaffected. Current relief pitchers could probably handle an increase in their workload by 30% to 40%, which is not inconsistent with the workload of relievers in the 70's.

Tango, Lichtman, and Dophin: page 234, The Book

CREATING THE LINE

When making your own baseball line, it is important to remember the old adage "Garbage in, Garbage out". If you use junk stats, you will end up with a junk number that is as good as flipping a coin to make your picks. Accurate power numbers on offense, defense and pitching are all needed to make a true, reliable line.

PYTHAGOREAN FORMULA

There are a variety of formulas that can be used to create a baseball line. The most common formula used is called the Pythagorean Theory. Bill James created Pythagorean; he used it to confirm his belief that the true measure of a team was its ratio between runs scored and runs allowed. James's initial formula was to square the total number of runs scored, then divide that number by the square of the number of runs allowed plus the square of the number of runs scored.

> WIN %= (RUNS FOR ^2)/((RUNS ALLOWED^2)+(RUNS FOR^2))

In Excel, the formula is written down as:

> =(POWER (A1, 2))/((POWER (A1, 2)+(POWER (B1, 2))))

Runs Scored equals A1, and Runs Allowed equals B1.

James later tweaked this formula slightly to make it even more accurate: instead of using two as the exponent, he used 1.83.

> **WIN %= (RUNS^1.83)/((RUNS ALLOWED^1.83)+(RUNS ^1.83))**

In a typical game, this was an extremely accurate barometer. In games where the run environment was higher (Texas) or lower (San Diego), however, the accuracy suffered.

THE DAVENPORT SOLUTION

Clay Davenport effectively solved this problem. His formula was similar to James:

> **WIN % = (RUNS ^EXPONENT) / ((RUNS ALLOWED^EXPONENT)+(RUNS^EXPONENT))**

The unique part of his method was the use of changing exponents to adapt to the run-scoring environment. Davenport first determined the run-scoring environment using this adjustment:

$$1.5 * \log \text{(expected runs per game for both teams)} +. 45$$

In Excel, Davenport's calculation is expressed as:

$$= 1.5*LOG (A1) + 0.45$$

A1 equals the total amount of runs expected for both teams.

This formula gives us different exponents depending on the run environment:

RUNS/ GAME	EXP	RUNS / GAME	EXP
1	0.450	9	1.881
2	0.902	10	1.950
3	1.166	11	2.012
4	1.353	12	2.069
5	1.498	13	2.121
6	1.617	14	2.169
7	1.718	15	2.214

Where James used just one number as the exponent, Davenport was able to adjust from game to game. It fixes the key flaw in formulas similar to James. In these cases, a team winning each game 6-3 will have an equal winning percentage as the team that typically wins each game 2-1. Since the Runs Scored/Runs Allowed ratio is the same, the winning percentage is the same.

Theoretically, this may make sense; reality dismisses such a belief. An outmatched basketball team will often slow down the tempo to shorten the game; the fewer possessions, the fewer chances for the better team to exploit its edge in talent. The same holds true in baseball. The lower amount of scoring, the more likely one fortunate play will determine the winner of the game.

In a typical run environment, a team expected to win 6-3 would have a 79% chance of winning the game. It is in the extreme run environments that Davenport's method makes its impact.

Using Davenport's method (written in Excel) you will see different winning percentages depending on the run environment:

Runs	Opp run	Tot Runs	Exponent
8	4	12	2.07
6	3	9	1.88
4	2	6	1.62
2	1	3	1.17

The variables above are translated into an expected winning percentage by using the following formula in Excel:

Formula in Excel	W %	Line
=Power(8,2.07)/((Power(8,2.07)+(Power(4,2.07))))	81%	-4.20
=Power(6,1.88)/((Power(6,1.88)+(Power(3,1.88))))	79%	-3.68
=Power(4,1.62)/((Power(4,1.62)+(Power(2,1.62))))	75%	-3.07
=Power(2,1.17)/((Power(2,1.17)+(Power(1,1.17))))	69%	-2.24

As a matter of practice, I prefer using the sports books Over/Under line to determine what exponent I use in Davenport's formula. Below is the list of exponents depending on the listed line:

Total	Exponent	Total	Exponent
6.5	1.67	10	1.95
7	1.72	10.5	1.98
7.5	1.76	11	2.01
8	1.8	11.5	2.04
8.5	1.84	12	2.07
9	1.88	12.5	2.1
9.5	1.92	13	2.12

PYTHAGENPAT

Another winning percentage estimator was developed by David Smith. It also uses a floating exponent that changes depending on the runs per game. In my experience it is slightly more accurate than the Davenport Solution; however I look at both when I am handicapping a game. The formula is a bit simpler than the Davenport solution:

EXPONENT= RUNS PER GAME ^ .287

WINNING %= RUNS ^ EXPONENT /
(RUNS ^ EXPONENT) + (RUNS ALLOWED ^ EXPONENT)

PUTTING IT ALL TOGETHER

So how does it all work? Let's use the September 28, 2007 game between the Florida Marlins and New York Mets. The Mets were in the midst of a historical collapse. With just seventeen games to go, New York had been a comfortable seven games in first place. A 4-10 stretch left the Mets tied with Philadelphia going into the final weekend of the season. Oliver Perez was on the mound for the Mets, facing Byung Hyun Kim of the Marlins. Florida, despite being on a four game winning streak, was 18 games behind the Mets and the Phillies in the division and suffering through a season from hell. New York was -200 favorite. The process below will detail just one method in creating your own line on a baseball game.

STEP 1: ESTIMATING EACH TEAM'S OFFENSE

The Florida Marlins on base average for the season is .337. Its slugging average was .450. Multiplying those two numbers will give me a .1516 OTS number. The average National League team has an on base average of .334 and a .423 slugging average. The league average OTS is .1413. Dividing the Marlins OTS number by the league average OTS will give me a 1.07 number; this means the Florida Marlins overall offense is 7% above league average.

The Marlins overall OTS number is just the starting point. I need to make possible adjustments. The Mets starter is a lefty; I want to see how well Florida hits lefties. Against left-handers, the Marlins splits are .345/.451. Those numbers average out to be about 10% above league average. The 3% difference seems significant, but it really isn't. Oliver Perez will be on a short hook tonight and may or may not reach the sixth inning. So while the Marlins hit lefties better than righties, the knowledge that the lefty may not be long for the game means I have to be careful when adjusting my power ratings based on the arm of the opposing pitcher.

There are other variables that I look at when making my offensive power ratings for a game. Home/away splits are important in some cases. How well a team has been hitting is relevant in others. Injuries, or players getting rest, matter at times also. In the case of this game, however, my concerns are limited. Florida has an offense about 8% above league average.

I go through the same process with the Mets. New York's batting splits are .342/.431; its OTS is .1474 compared to the .1412 league average. After dividing those two numbers, I get New York's basic offensive power rating is 1.04. A right-hander is on the mound for Florida; New York has hit about 9% higher than league average against righties on the season. Byung-Hyun Kim is also one of those pitchers that have huge platoon splits. These two splits mean I need to increase the Mets' power rating. Shea Stadium plays a role as well, decreasing run scoring by about 5% over the course of the season. Taking these additional factors into consideration, I make New York's offensive power rating about a 1.10. The Marlins' offensive rating is 1.08.

STEP 2: ESTIMATING THE PITCHING

Kim was one of the worst pitchers in the National League in the 2007 season. Starting the season with the Colorado Rockies, Kim also saw time with the Marlins and the Arizona. He moved into the starting rotation for Florida in September and had gotten rocked in his previous five starts. I looked at a variety of numbers to help me determine how well Kim was expected to throw.

- Season ERA: 6.09
- September ERA: 7.50
- xERA: 5.42
- FIP ERA: 5.41
- Q-ERA: 4.91

Kim had been striking out batters at the league average rate, but couldn't consistently throw strikes and was getting lit up because of it. Using the above information, I expected Kim to have a 5.70 ERA in about five innings of work. Against a league average offense, Kim would allow 3.17 runs in those five innings of work.

The other four innings of work was going to be thrown by the Marlins bullpen. Florida's pen had struggled at times, and I made its power rating for the bullpen at about 8% worse than average. Since the average ERA in the National League is 4.43, Florida's bullpen ERA is given a 4.78 rating. They will allow 2.13 runs in the final four innings of the game. All told, the Marlins pitching would allow 5.30 runs versus a league average offense. If I divide 5.3 runs by 4.43 (average NL ERA), I get a pitching power rating of 1.20 for the Marlins. Florida's pitching performance will theoretically be 20% worse than the league average.

I now do the same for the Mets. Oliver Perez has these numbers:

- Season ERA: 3.56
- September ERA: 2.88
- xERA: 3.94
- FIP ERA: 3.32
- Q-ERA: 4.15

Perez's September ERA was helped by the fact he allowed six unearned runs that month. He had been throwing OK but wasn't dominating like his FIP ERA and September ERA indicate. I gave him a rating of 4.00 ERA in seven innings pitched. Against a league average team, Perez would be expected to allow 3.1 runs in seven innings of work.

New York's bullpen would carry the load the final two innings. The Mets raw numbers indicate a powerful bullpen. It wasn't at the time. The pen was exhausted and a key factor of its late season collapse. I judge New York's bullpen at slightly below average. I don't use that number, however. Since Perez is expected to go seven innings, a rested Aaron Heilman and Billy Wagner should close out the game. Those two are high quality pitchers, and I give the Mets pen a rating about 5% better than average. They will allow .93 runs over the final two innings. For the game, the Marlins would be expected to score 4.03 runs in this game. I divide that number by 4.43 (average NL ERA) to get a 91% power rating.

STEP 3: EXPECTED RUNS SCORED

To determine the number of runs a team can be expected to score, simply multiply a team's offensive power rating by its opponent's pitching rating, and then multiply that number by the average runs scored in the league.

Florida Offense rating (1.08) * Mets Pitching rating (.91) * 4.71
Florida is expected to score 4.63 runs in an average ballpark.

Mets offense rating (1.10) * Florida Pitching rating (1.20) * 4.71
New York should score 6.22 runs in a league average park.

STEP 4: DETERMINE EXPECTED WINNING PERCENTAGE

The Total is set at 9.5, meaning the exponent in the Davenport Solution is 1.916. The formula in Excel will look like this:

=Power (6.22, 1.916) / ((Power (4.63, 1.916) + (Power (6.22, 1.916))

New York's expected winning percentage, before home field advantage is considered, is 64% for a true line of -1.76. Florida's line would be the opposite: they would be priced at 1.76.

STEP 5: HOME FIELD ADVANTAGE ADJUSTMENTS

The Mets collapse had mostly taken place at Shea Stadium; New York was riding a seven game home losing streak coming into the September 28th game. The late season pressure was getting to the Mets, and playing at home obviously was making matters worse. In May, I had given New York sixteen cents on the money line in a series between these two same teams. I couldn't do that for this series. There was no home field advantage. In fact, I could make a good argument that I needed to adjust the Mets down for playing at home. My price: Mets -1.76.

Now the handicapping really begins. Have the Mets regrouped after blowing a division lead that they held for five months? Does Florida care about the game, or are they going through the motions at the end of the season? Is Florida going to play its key players? How overworked is the Marlins bullpen? There are many variables that need to be examined before betting the game. Creating your own line only indicates possible plays. Don't make it out to be any more than that. All these intangibles, and the nice price, pointed towards Florida in this game.

So how did the game end up? Kim gave up four runs in five innings. The Marlins bullpen was surprisingly effective: the four relievers shut out the Mets and allowed just four hits. The Mets pen was strong as well, allowing only one run in over five innings of work. The problem for New York was its starter. Oliver Perez didn't make it out of the fourth inning, getting hammered for six runs and dropping the Mets out its first place tie with Philadelphia. Florida 7, New York 4. For all intents and purposes, the Mets' season was over.

THE PHYSICS OF BASEBALL

The role of physics and the environment is rarely mentioned in baseball, but it can be a major factor when betting a game. Some effects are obvious, such as the increased scoring at Coors Field or the lowered run totals when the wind is blowing in. However, other effects are a bit subtler. Game-time temperature, barometric pressure, and humidity all are possible influences on an individual baseball game. Dr. Robert Adair, Professor of Physics at Yale, was asked by Commissioner Bart Giamatti to study the elements of baseball that are affected by physics. The book that followed Adair's research is both a fascinating read and a valuable resource in handicapping, particularly when you play totals.

Coors Field, Altitude's Poster Child

Prior the 2006 season, the ball would fly out of Coors Field in Colorado, leaving pitchers shell-shocked and hitters rich. At times, the total couldn't be set high enough; 13 was a common number bookmakers post in order to split the action. High altitude was given most of the blame for the high scoring in Denver.

The more you rise above sea level, the less dense air is. Air density plays a key factor in determining how far a batted ball travels, how fast it travels, and how much it moves when it travels.

These reasons conspire to make Coors a hitter's paradise. A curve ball that might drop 8 inches more (in comparison to a fastball) will drop only four inches because of the thin air. It also will break less because it crosses home plate faster; the ball doesn't have time to break the way it would at sea level. A fastball is 6 inches quicker in Coors than at Shea Stadium. That may be good for a pitcher in theory, but the batter will gladly trade a slightly faster pitch for less movement.

The defense suffers as well from the low density. Outfielders, already having problems handling the vast expanse of the Rockies outfield, discovered that balls hit into the gap at Coors fly further and land quicker. This costs a typical outfielder eight to nine feet in range. An infielder also loses range. Adair estimates that a shortstop loses about a foot in range because of the low air density, a significant amount in this game of inches.

In recent years, the Rockies management has taken a few steps to downplay this environmental pollution. The most publicized is the use of a humidor, a device that will keep the balls out of the dry Colorado air until game time. The humidor is set for 70 degrees with 50 % humidity, the same specifications used by the Rawlings plant in St. Louis. The ball is slightly heavier, plus it is much easier for a pitcher to grip. Mike Dejean of Colorado says that before the humidor, the leather would crack because the ball would get so dry. "That's why we were always licking our fingers. You couldn't feel the seams. It was like throwing a cue ball. Now the leather is supple. You can grip the ball and really throw your breaking pitches."

Another method was the manipulation of the ballpark grass. A once lightning fast infield has been slowed considerably simply because the Rockies groundskeepers are letting the grass grow longer. Initially, these steps seemed to have worked. In 2006, a number of articles were written detailing the sudden drop in scoring at Coors Field. Only 9.1 runs per game were being scored in Denver from the start of the season until the end of July. The game went Under 69% of the time in those games.

Then August came. By this time the sports books had already adjusted to the new Coors, usually putting the total at 9 or 9.5 runs. Coors Field, however, reverted back to form. An average of 10.7 runs was scored per game in August in Denver. The games went under in just four of 14 games. September came and the offensive explosion continued. 12.7 runs per game were scored in September. This time only one of the thirteen games in Coors went Under the total. The old monster had once again reared its head.

Coors is the best known for altitude effects, but many other stadiums in baseball are impacted as well. These parks obviously don't have the elevation of Coors, but they still show considerable differences when compared to 'sea-level' parks.

Adair estimates that a ball hit 400 feet in San Francisco would travel an additional seven feet every 1000 feet in elevation. The same ball hit in Pittsburgh would fly about 408 feet. In Atlanta the ball would go about 407 feet. In Detroit, it would travel 404 feet. Altitude matters. The chart below shows the impact on a 400-foot fly ball for each stadium.

TEAM	ALTITUDE	DIST	TEAM	ALT	DIST
Anaheim	160	401	Milwaukee	635	404
Arizona	1090	408	Minnesota	815	406
Atlanta	1050	407	Yankees	55	400
Baltimore	20	400	Mets	55	400
Boston	21	400	Oakland	25	400
Chi Cubs	595	404	Philly	5	400
White Sox	595	404	Pittsburgh	730	405
Cincinnati	550	404	San Diego	13	400

Cleveland	777	405	Seattle	400	403
Colorado	5280	437	San Fran	75	401
Detroit	633	404	St Louis	455	403
Florida	10	400	Tampa Bay	15	400
Houston	22	400	Texas	551	404
Kansas City	750	405	Toronto	300	402
Los Angeles	340	402	Washington	25	400

Ball Temperature

The temperature of game ball affects the game as well. Softball players have been known to put game balls in the microwave before playing a game; how long this nuked ball stays hot is hard to tell but the theory behind the action is correct. Each 10-degree increase in ball temperature will result in the 400-foot fly ball traveling an additional 4 feet. Warning track power on a normal ball may be a home run with a ball 10 degrees hotter.

Old timers tell stories about John McGraw storing balls in an icebox, to be used only when the visiting team is at the plate. This might have worked years ago, but MLB has since changed the rules and dictated that all balls used in the game must be supplied to the umpires two hours before game time.

Game Time Temperature

The hotter the day, the farther the ball goes. If it is hot outside, the ball temperature naturally tends to rise as well. Air density is also reduced. For each 10-degree rise in heat, the 400-foot drive hit at sea level would go four feet further. Hot days lead to more runs. As a rule of thumb, add ½ run to your own total number if the game time temperature is over 90 degrees. If it is below 55 degrees, subtract ½ run from your total. Pay close attention to the home plate umpire however. More than a few will widen the strike zone if they don't like the weather.

GAME TIME TEMPERATURE	RUNS/GAME
Greater than 90 degrees	11.2
Between 80-89 degrees	10.3
Between 70-79 degrees	10.0
Between 56-69 degrees	9.4
Below 56 degrees	8.9

Barometer

When barometric pressure is lower, so is the air resistance to a ball in flight. Each 1-inch drop in barometric pressure results in a six-foot increase in the length of a 400-foot fly ball.

Humidity

The heavier the ball, the less distance it will travel. A ball stored at 100% humidity for four weeks will weigh 11% more than a typical ball. The 'bounce' of the ball is also affected. The humidity ball will travel 30 feet less than a ball stored at low humidity. This effect may have merit at Coors, which began storing their balls in a humidifier in 2003. For the most part, however, the game time humidity has little bearing on the number of runs scored in a game. Jan Null, director of meteorology for Planetweather.com, says this about humidity and its effect on a baseball:

"The air is approximately 21 percent oxygen, 78 percent nitrogen and some very small amounts of other gases. Now if we look at the weight of the molecules (i.e., molecular weight) of dry air we see it has a value of 29. But gaseous water vapor has a molecular weight of only 18. Because the air around us is a mixture of dry air and water vapor, its actual molecular weight falls somewhere between 18 and 29, with it being less on humid days. When the air becomes more humid, its density lessens, so it creates less drag or friction, which would slow a baseball or allow it to curve.

However, the dynamics aren't quite that simple because high humidity can cause a baseball to gain a small amount of water, which makes it slightly heavier. The bottom line is that the effect of humidity, all other things being equal, is negligible."

Wind

The first thing a better does each morning is to check the weather report at Wrigley Field. Wind blowing in off the lake means a low total; wind blowing out means the opposite. Each one-mph increase in wind adds three feet to a 400-foot drive. However, that is a bit misleading. A 400-foot drive with 20-mph wind blowing out to left field won't go 460 feet. All stadiums have grandstands acting as wind blocks; the 20-mph wind to center field may only be five mph around home plate. Once the ball gets up in the air, the wind will take over. But generally, most batted balls aren't as affected as they would be if the wind were blowing in.

A hidden effect of the wind may occur to the pitcher as well. Wind doesn't affect fastballs; the average fastball traveling 90 mph crosses home plate .4 seconds after the ball is released. If a 10-mph wind is blowing in the pitcher's face, that 90 mph pitch will only slow down to 89 mph.

However, wind creates havoc with off-speed pitches. In the case of crosswinds, a curve ball may break as many as 21 inches or as few as 8 inches. Gusty days can plays havoc on pitchers who must locate their off-speed pitches. Pay close attention to wind speed when a finesse pitcher is on the mound.

Defense is also affected by wind. Wind-blown pop-ups and fly balls often fall between defensive players, resulting in an unfair hit being charged to the pitcher. Some stadiums are effective in blocking wind. Others just make it swirl, causing havoc for everyone involved. The numbers below show the effects of heavy wind in comparison to extremely slight/still wind.

WIND SPEED	Gms	ERRORS/Gm	RUNS/GM	BB/GM	K'S/GM
Over 20 MPH	290	1.52	10.8	7.37	12.83
2 MPH or less	234	1.47	10.4	6.73	12.39

The wind has more of an impact on day games than games in the evening. If the weather sites show heavy winds during the day, don't assume it will keep blowing for a night game. Wind also blows harder in April and May. Once summer hits, the wind doesn't affect nearly as many ballgames as it they did early in the season. Below are the wind charts for cities with outdoor stadiums. This likely goes into the "too much information" category, but here it is nonetheless.

TEAM	April	May	June	July	Aug	Sept	Oct
Arizona	6.9	7	6.7	7.1	6.6	6.3	5.8
Atlanta	10.1	8.7	8.1	7.7	7.3	8	8.5
Baltimore	10.2	8.9	8.2	7.6	7.5	7.7	8.1
Boston	13.1	12	11.4	11	10.8	11.3	11.9
Chicago	11.9	10.5	9.3	8.4	8.2	8.9	10.1
Cincinnati	10.6	8.7	7.9	7.2	6.8	7.4	8.1
Cleveland	11.5	10	9.2	8.6	8.2	8.9	9.9
Colorado	10	9.3	8.8	8.3	8	7.9	7.8
Detroit	11.3	10.1	9.2	8.5	8.1	8.7	9.7
Florida	10.5	9.5	8.3	7.9	7.9	8.2	9.2

Kansas City	12.3	10.3	9.9	9.2	8.8	9.6	10.5
Los Angeles	8.5	8.4	8	7.9	7.7	7.3	6.9
Milwaukee	12.8	11.5	10.4	9.7	9.5	10.4	11.4
New York	12.9	11.6	11	10.4	10.3	11	11.6
Philadelphia	10.8	9.5	8.8	8.2	8	8.3	8.8
Pittsburgh	10.2	8.7	8	7.3	6.8	7.4	8.3
San Diego	7.8	7.9	7.8	7.5	7.4	7.1	6.5
San Francisco	12.2	13.4	14	13.6	12.8	11.1	9.4
St. Louis	11.3	9.4	8.8	8	7.6	8.2	8.9
Texas	12.4	11.1	10.6	9.8	8.9	9.3	9.7

PARK EFFECTS

A home run hit in Coors Field is not equal to a homer hit in Dodger Stadium. This concept, known as the park effect, states that statistics like runs, ERA, batting average and so on, are all dependent in part on the environment of a specific park. Coors Field has been the most hitter friendly park in baseball the last few years, followed by the Ballpark in Arlington, Chase Field in Arizona, and Citizens Bank Park in Philadelphia. Pitchers from these teams are generally better than a number like ERA indicates, and the offense in comparison isn't quite as powerful as one might suspect.

There are several methods a handicapper can use to establish a team's true park factor. Base Park Index is the simplest; it involves eight steps:

Calculating Park Factors	
Step 1	Add The Total Runs Scored In Home Park
Step 2	Add The Total At-Bats In Home Park
Step 3	Divide Step 1 By Step 2
Step 4	Add The Total Runs Scored In Away Games
Step 5	Add The Total At-Bats In Away Games
Step 6	Divide Step 4 By Step 5
Step 7	Divide Step 5 By Step 6

This typically gives a number ranging from 90% to 110%. If a ballpark's number is 100%, then it is a league average park. A 110% number means that it is a hitter's park; there are 10% more runs scored at that stadium than a league average park. A 90% number means the park has decreased scoring by 10%.

It is advisable to calculate park factors for more than one year; random fluctuations will often play havoc with your park factors if you use only one year. Five-year data pools tend to be the most accurate. Many handicappers, however, believe three years' worth of data will tend to smooth out the chance factor. Weather fluctuates from year to year. An unusually hot and dry summer will increase scoring. Wind patterns shift from year to year as well. These are just a few examples as to what may adversely affect the accuracy of Park Factors.

It is also a reason why precision regarding park factors isn't necessary or even wanted. A bettor should go into each day's game with an open mind as to how that park will play that game. If the wind is kicking up, or a cold streak coming through town, that five-year data pool doesn't mean much.

Park factors help filter out the bias that a team has from playing in an extreme pitcher/hitter park. It is only a tool, however, and not a totally accurate one at that. AT&T Park may depress home runs from left-handed hitters overall, but Barry Bonds certainly wasn't affected too much by his home park.

A good example of the strangeness of park factors is the Sportsman's Park experience. Bill Febler, in "The Book on the Book", details this story. Before moving to Baltimore, the St. Louis Browns shared Sportsman's Park with the St. Louis Cardinals. Since both teams shared the same stadium, one would assume that the park factor would be generally the same. Not true. In the 33 years that the two teams shared the stadium, the Browns had a park factor of 114%. The Cardinals' park factor was only 107%.

The numbers varied widely when looking at specific years. In 1920, the Cardinals had a 99% park factor. The Browns saw an increase of scoring by 24%, one of the best offensive parks in the American League. The 33-year history saw other similar occurrences. In 1938, the Cardinals had a park factor of 138%. The Browns' park factor was only 104%.

This wasn't just limited to St. Louis. When the Yankees and Mets shared Shea Stadium for two years in the 1970's, the home park factors for each team varied widely. The Phillies and A's saw similar results when those two clubs shared the same park. Park factors aren't perfect, and be cautious before relying on them. But don't discount it. This 'best guess' tool is a valuable piece of handicapping.

If Petco Field in San Diego deflates run scoring by 25%, then the park factor is listed as 75%. To adjust a Padres pitcher's stats for park factor, you will have to divide its run inflation rate (-24%) by 2 to account for the fact that the player plays half his games at home.

For example, Kevin Correia had a 3.91 ERA last year pitching for San Diego. Accounting for San Diego's 75% park factor would show Correia's adjusted ERA to be 4.40.

Step 1:	75% - 1
Step 2:	Divide Step 1 by Step 2 = -12.5%
Step 3:	Step 2 * 3.91
Step 4:	4.14 – Step 3

These adjustments aren't perfect, and a bettor shouldn't always trust the numbers. The unbalanced schedule throws a wrench into these calculations as well. It is, however, a reasonable way to judge how the perception of a pitcher may be wrong because of that pitcher's home ball park.

What makes a park effect?

1) Dimensions of the park
2) Visibility and hitting background
3) Size of foul territory
4) Playing surface
5) Climate
6) Altitude

BALLPARK LAYOUTS

Knowing which way the wind is blowing can help a bettor decide which way to bet a total. The diagrams below shows how each stadium is laid out. The bottom of the diagram shows south; the right side is east, the left side is west, and the top is north. Wind blowing straight from the north in Anaheim will be blowing in from left field. Wind blowing from the west will be blowing out to right field.

CHASE FIELD, ARIZONA

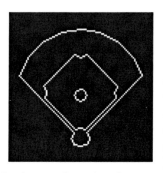

Due to the Arizona heat, Chase Field's roof typically is closed during the summer while the air conditioning is kept going full speed. With the roof shut and the air conditioning running, the ball doesn't carry as well. When the roof is open, runs will score often. Even when closed, however, the stadium is a hitter's ballpark. Chase Field has an elevation 1,100 above sea level, the second highest stadium in the majors behind Coors Field in Denver. The high altitude and a great hitter's background are big factors in the high number of runs scored in Chase. Home runs are plentiful here, and fly-ball pitchers can struggle.

PARK NAME	Year	RUNS	HR	H	2B	3B	BB
Chase Field	2005	109%	105%	105%	108%	162%	105%
Chase Field	2006	114%	134%	110%	110%	164%	108%
Chase Field	2007	111%	111%	105%	108%	252%	107%
Chase Field	2008	114%	107%	107%	124%	141%	96%
Chase Field	2009	119%	104%	109%	130%	156%	100%
5 Year Average		113%	112%	107%	116%	175%	103%

Year	Over	Under	Push	Over %	Under %	RF	RA
2005	36	42	3	46%	54%	4.5	4.7
2006	40	39	2	51%	49%	4.2	5.5
2007	41	38	2	52%	48%	5.0	5.3
2008	44	37	4	54%	46%	4.7	4.6
2009	41	36	4	53%	47%	4.8	4.5
	202	192	15	49%	47%	4.6	4.9

TURNER FIELD, ATLANTA

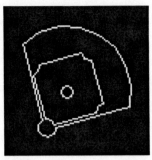

Turner Field was originally built as the main stadium for the 1996 Olympic Games in Atlanta. Once the Games were over, the Braves converted the stadium into a modern day ballpark with suites and luxury boxes. Turner Field isn't the Launching Pad II; it is now a pitcher friendly park that hurts left-handed power hitters and teams that don't have quick outfielders in center and right field. Andruw Jones was outstanding here. Winds and cool air can keep scoring down in the spring, but the high altitude and wind blowing through the open centerfield area will help the ball carry on warmer days.

PARK NAME	Year	RUNS	HR	H	2B	3B	BB
Turner Field	2005	109%	88%	105%	112%	136%	101%
Turner Field	2006	95%	93%	103%	99%	72%	91%
Turner Field	2007	91%	96%	91%	77%	89%	111%
Turner Field	2008	106%	101%	107%	103%	121%	111%
Turner Field	2009	90%	86%	94%	85%	109%	107%
5 Year Average		98%	93%	100%	95%	105%	104%

Year	Over	Under	Push	Over %	Under %	RF	RA
2005	39	40	4	49%	51%	4.3	4.3
2006	37	42	5	47%	53%	4.8	4.3
2007	47	30	4	61%	39%	5.1	4.8
2008	37	39	5	49%	51%	4.7	4.4
2009	40	39	2	51%	49%	4.7	5.0
	200	190	20	49%	46%	4.7	4.6

CAMDEN YARDS, BALTIMORE

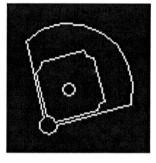

Camden Yards set the standard when it comes to new baseball stadiums. Built in 1992, Camden is generally a pitcher's friend. The 25-foot high wall in right field will knock down a lot of potential homeruns, although the ball does tend to carry a bit when the weather heats up. Baltimore typically grows the infield grass higher than most ballparks, helping ground ball pitchers as well as teams with infielders that may be lacking in range. Right handed batters love taking a shot at the 364-foot fence in left center.

PARK NAME	Year	RUNS	HR	H	2B	3B	BB
Camden Yards	2005	88%	95%	94%	83%	69%	121%
Camden Yards	2006	99%	118%	103%	88%	60%	91%
Camden Yards	2007	111%	123%	110%	96%	135%	99%
Camden Yards	2008	105%	136%	104%	99%	57%	95%
Camden Yards	2009	104%	119%	111%	98%	104%	93%
5 Year Average		101%	118%	105%	93%	85%	100%

Year	Over	Under	Push	Over %	Under %	RF	RA
2005	37	39	5	49%	51%	4.9	5.1
2006	45	30	6	60%	40%	5.1	5.6
2007	43	38	0	53%	47%	5.1	5.1
2008	45	33	3	58%	42%	4.8	5.8
2009	38	36	6	51%	49%	5.0	5.5
	208	176	20	51%	44%	5.0	5.4

FENWAY PARK, BOSTON

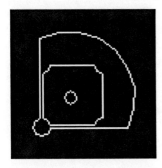

There are no cheap outs in Fenway. The small foul grounds and short field means a pitcher cannot make a mistake without paying for it. It also means foul pop flies are now caught by fans rather than players in the field. The 17-foot wall in centerfield also helps out hitters by providing a great hitting background. Then you have the Green Monster, which turns routing fly balls into extra-base hits. It is deadly to a left-handed junk baller. Pitchers who get their own outs via the strikeout will do better in this ballpark than a control pitcher who must rely on his defense to get him out of trouble. Lefties have always had a tough time hitting home runs in Fenway. What is new is the difficulties right-handed hitters have recently had hitting the long ball. Power from RHers has taken a dive since the 2006 season. What's changed? Stadium renovation may have messed with the wind currents. Time will tell.

PARK NAME	Year	RUNS	HR	H	2B	3B	BB
Fenway Park	2005	103%	89%	97%	132%	88%	108%
Fenway Park	2006	103%	73%	104%	137%	100%	94%
Fenway Park	2007	118%	88%	114%	135%	96%	95%
Fenway Park	2008	108%	85%	106%	159%	100%	110%
Fenway Park	2009	107%	96%	99%	137%	108%	88%
5 Year Average		108%	86%	104%	140%	98%	99%

Year	Over	Under	Push	Over %	Under %	RF	RA
2005	39	39	5	50%	50%	5.3	5.2
2006	52	31	4	63%	37%	6.4	5.0
2007	42	34	5	55%	45%	5.2	5.1
2008	47	35	7	57%	43%	6.0	4.2
2009	39	43	4	48%	52%	5.6	4.3
	219	182	25	51%	43%	5.7	4.8

CELLULAR ONE, CHICAGO WHITE SOX

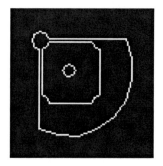

The Cell has undergone major renovations the last few years to fix some of the horrible mistakes that occurred when the stadium was being designed and built in the early 90's. The upper deck was reworked in 2004, playing havoc with wind conditions at times. It is now a power park: home runs are extremely common since the White Sox moved the fences in after the 2000 season. The infield is usually in good shape. Fly-ball pitchers dread this place.

PARK NAME	Year	RUNS	HR	H	2B	3B	BB
Cellular Field	2005	105%	138%	98%	92%	84%	108%
Cellular Field	2006	105%	131%	101%	91%	65%	112%
Cellular Field	2007	108%	122%	103%	99%	47%	97%
Cellular Field	2008	112%	135%	97%	91%	56%	109%
Cellular Field	2009	106%	119%	96%	92%	79%	113%
5 Year Average		107%	129%	99%	93%	66%	108%

Year	Over	Under	Push	Over %	Under %	RF	RA
2005	34	50	3	41%	60%	4.7	3.6
2006	48	31	2	61%	39%	5.8	5.4
2007	41	37	3	53%	47%	5.7	4.8
2008	36	39	6	48%	52%	4.3	5.5
2009	44	38	2	54%	46%	5.7	4.2
	203	195	16	49%	47%	5.2	4.7

WRIGLEY FIELD, CHICAGO CUBS

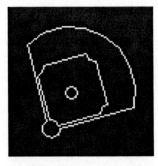 Just look to the weather to decide how Wrigley Field is going to play. When the wind blows off the lake, scoring is down. When it blows out, the scoring soars. The problem with Wrigley Field weather is everyone knows about it. When the wind is blowing in, the line typically is set way too low to take advantage of the wind. Often times the value is taking the Over when the wind is blowing in, and the Under when the wind is blowing out. The Cubs have done some work on the park in recent years, adding seats on the 3rd base line, lowering the field 14 inches (making fences higher in the process) and adding seats in the outfield bleachers. These changes may affect how the park plays so it is something to keep an eye on over the season.

PARK NAME	Year	RUNS	HR	H	2B	3B	BB
Wrigley Field	2005	101%	105%	101%	106%	110%	96%
Wrigley Field	2006	108%	121%	101%	108%	136%	90%
Wrigley Field	2007	117%	115%	108%	120%	90%	111%
Wrigley Field	2008	107%	116%	103%	98%	66%	94%
Wrigley Field	2009	115%	101%	102%	105%	92%	104%
5 Year Average		109%	112%	103%	107%	99%	99%

Year	Over	Under	Push	Over %	Under %	RF	RA
2005	36	41	4	47%	53%	4.3	4.4
2006	38	43	1	47%	53%	5.2	4.3
2007	40	32	9	56%	44%	4.6	5.3
2008	40	40	2	50%	50%	5.0	4.6
2009	41	40	2	51%	49%	5.5	4.3
	195	196	18	48%	48%	4.9	4.6

GREAT AMERICAN BALLPARK, CINCINNATI

The Great American Ballpark is a good reason why 5-year park factors are the best way to determine the true run environment of a stadium. Its first two seasons, Great American Ballpark played as a pitcher's park.. Since then, it has been all hitters thriving here. Johnny Cueto and other fly-ball pitchers walk a fine line in this stadium due to its small fences. Pay close attention to the weather; this is one of those major league stadiums where the scoring is heavily impacted by weather conditions. Run scoring was down last year, despite the home run rate remaining high compared to league average. Expect more scoring in 2010.

PARK NAME	Year	RUNS	HR	H	2B	3B	BB
Great American Ball Park	2005	113%	125%	106%	118%	54%	96%
Great American Ball Park	2006	115%	128%	103%	93%	40%	107%
Great American Ball Park	2007	110%	135%	97%	105%	82%	104%
Great American Ball Park	2008	107%	123%	101%	102%	104%	101%
Great American Ball Park	2009	98%	118%	100%	102%	109%	104%
5 Year Average		108%	126%	101%	104%	78%	102%

Year	Over	Under	Push	Over %	Under %	RF	RA
2005	38	39	4	49%	51%	4.6	5.3
2006	35	44	2	44%	56%	4.1	5.2
2007	42	36	3	54%	46%	5.0	5.3
2008	41	33	7	55%	45%	5.1	5.4
2009	37	36	8	51%	49%	4.7	4.9
	193	188	24	48%	46%	4.7	5.2

JACOBS FIELD, CLEVELAND

Teams loaded with left-handed bats can have a slight advantage at Jacobs Field, especially in warmer weather when the wind blows out. The 17-foot fence in left field often helps lefties on the mound, but the short distance from home plate makes fly ball pitchers vulnerable. Scoring had increased in 2007 and 2008, but those years look to be flukes compared to other years. In 2009, runs were scored at just 84% of the league average. Bookmakers know all about it, however. Games went over 53% of the time despite the lack of runs scoring at Jacobs.

PARK NAME	Year	RUNS	HR	H	2B	3B	BB
Progressive Field	2005	87%	87%	92%	104%	36%	100%
Progressive Field	2006	95%	87%	94%	98%	79%	107%
Progressive Field	2007	112%	110%	103%	88%	65%	105%
Progressive Field	2008	100%	82%	102%	102%	65%	119%
Progressive Field	2009	84%	67%	96%	101%	53%	95%
5 Year Average		95%	87%	98%	99%	60%	105%

Year	Over	Under	Push	Over %	Under %	RF	RA
2005	39	39	3	50%	50%	5.2	4.2
2006	36	43	2	46%	54%	5.1	5.3
2007	37	38	6	49%	51%	5.4	4.5
2008	39	43	3	48%	52%	5.3	4.5
2009	42	38	1	53%	48%	5.3	4.4
	193	201	15	47%	49%	5.3	4.6

COORS FIELD, DENVER

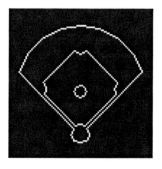

A team will struggle if it doesn't have quick outfielders in Coors. The deep fences are needed to keep Denver's high altitude from turning into a baseball game. Deeper fences mean more gaps, and pitchers that can't create their own outs via strikeouts typically struggle. Walks are a killer in Coors. Avoid pitchers who can't throw strikes. Right-handed batters thrive in this park. Scoring is trending down due to external factors like the humidifier and higher grass in the playing field. Be careful here. While still a great offensive park, the tricks being played by MLB to lower run scoring here can be tough to analyze. Home runs dropped sharply last year compared to previous seasons, but scoring remained high as triples, doubles and walks increased.

PARK NAME	Year	RUNS	HR	H	2B	3B	BB
Coors Field	2005	128%	110%	125%	114%	144%	104%
Coors Field	2006	115%	117%	114%	101%	122%	107%
Coors Field	2007	116%	122%	112%	126%	151%	94%
Coors Field	2008	113%	130%	110%	105%	139%	92%
Coors Field	2009	125%	108%	116%	127%	177%	107%
5 Year Average		119%	117%	115%	114%	147%	101%

Year	Over	Under	Push	Over %	Under %	RF	RA
2005	38	41	2	48%	52%	3.6	5.1
2006	38	39	4	49%	51%	6.1	6.6
2007	38	41	2	48%	52%	5.6	5.1
2008	45	41	1	52%	48%	5.7	4.8
2009	36	41	4	47%	53%	5.1	5.2
	195	203	13	47%	49%	5.2	5.4

COMERICA PARK, DETROIT

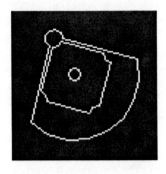

Comerica was once a pitcher's best friend. That has changed over the last three seasons. The main reason for the change was the increase of home runs; the home run rate was 15% above league average in 2007 and 2008. While that rate dropped back last season, runs still scored at above the league average in 2009. Over has hit 57% of the time in the last two seasons. Speed is valuable in Comerica, particularly in the outfield.

PARK NAME	Year	RUNS	HR	H	2B	3B	BB
Comerica Park	2005	96%	94%	104%	89%	176%	105%
Comerica Park	2006	98%	81%	102%	92%	117%	102%
Comerica Park	2007	105%	114%	100%	97%	160%	106%
Comerica Park	2008	108%	119%	107%	97%	111%	88%
Comerica Park	2009	103%	97%	96%	95%	108%	103%
5 Year Average		102%	101%	102%	94%	134%	101%

Year	Over	Under	Push	Over %	Under %	RF	RA
2005	37	40	4	48%	52%	4.4	5.1
2006	39	39	3	50%	50%	4.7	5.2
2007	37	46	4	45%	55%	4.8	4.2
2008	44	31	6	59%	41%	5.5	5.1
2009	41	35	5	54%	46%	5.4	5.3
	198	191	22	48%	46%	5.0	5.0

SUN LIFE STADIUM, FLORIDA

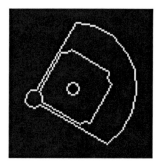

There is a lot of wide open space in Sun Life Stadium. Speedy contact hitters can thrive here. It is difficult to hit home runs, and the lightning fast grass leads to a ton of triples in this park. Defense is a key here. Right field is extremely large and a quick right fielder will help a pitcher. Fly-ball pitchers do well in this park.; leaving the ball up often just results in 400 foot outs. The Teal Monster, a 33-foot high wall in left field, also knocks down potential home runs from right-handed hitters. Lefties have it a little easier however. The increase in home runs in 2009 was most likely a fluke.

PARK NAME	Year	RUNS	HR	H	2B	3B	BB
Land Shark Stadium	2005	89%	81%	93%	86%	111%	112%
Land Shark Stadium	2006	90%	88%	95%	97%	141%	111%
Land Shark Stadium	2007	107%	101%	103%	115%	146%	115%
Land Shark Stadium	2008	95%	84%	95%	93%	148%	103%
Land Shark Stadium	2009	114%	113%	108%	111%	64%	114%
5 Year Average		99%	93%	99%	100%	122%	111%

Year	Over	Under	Push	Over %	Under %	RF	RA
2005	44	33	4	57%	43%	4.6	4.9
2006	33	37	8	47%	53%	4.1	4.1
2007	41	38	2	52%	48%	4.4	4.6
2008	48	29	4	62%	38%	5.0	5.7
2009	38	39	4	49%	51%	4.6	4.8
	204	176	22	51%	44%	4.5	4.8

MINUTE MAID PARK, HOUSTON

The 2005 World Series seemed to be more of a battle between Bud Selig and the Houston Astros rather than White Sox vs. Houston. Selig got his way, the roof stayed open, and Chicago won both games in Houston. Astros players love playing with the roof closed; even on nice days, the roof remains closed. When the roof is closed, the air conditioning takes over and keeps the ball from carrying as it does on those rare occasions where it is open. The park plays small at times; home runs into the left field stands are fly-ball outs in most stadiums. The huge center field does help make up for the short fences down the corners. Lefty pull hitters see their power numbers fall; right-handers enjoy a left field that drastically inflates their power numbers.

PARK NAME	Year	RUNS	HR	H	2B	3B	BB
Minute Maid Park	2005	95%	119%	99%	80%	91%	96%
Minute Maid Park	2006	103%	117%	99%	101%	129%	97%
Minute Maid Park	2007	90%	105%	100%	93%	123%	99%
Minute Maid Park	2008	104%	116%	101%	110%	91%	100%
Minute Maid Park	2009	93%	107%	104%	87%	100%	97%
5 Year Average		97%	113%	101%	94%	107%	98%

Year	Over	Under	Push	Over %	Under %	RF	RA
2005	41	46	2	47%	53%	4.1	4.1
2006	42	41	3	51%	49%	5.0	4.2
2007	36	36	9	50%	50%	4.6	4.5
2008	36	42	3	46%	54%	4.5	4.5
2009	34	40	4	46%	54%	4.7	4.6
	189	205	21	46%	49%	4.6	4.4

KAUFFMAN STADIUM, KANSAS CITY

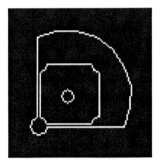 Kauffman Stadium was built in 1973 and is still one of the better parks in baseball. Weather effects are important here. In the springtime, the wind often comes in from the north, keeping scores down. Once the temperature heats up, however, so does the scoring. On hot days, the ball flies all over the park. From 1995 to 2003, the Royals had quietly played in one of the great offensive parks in baseball. In 2004, however, Kansas City moved its fences back 10 feet and the results were startling. It is extremely difficult to hit home runs in Kaufman. Increases in doubles and triples help make up the difference; other than a small blip in 2008, scoring is above league average. Renovations to the ball park were completed prior to the 2009 season, so the park factor is still not set in stone.

PARK NAME	Year	RUNS	HR	H	2B	3B	BB
Kauffman Stadium	2005	97%	76%	102%	116%	90%	99%
Kauffman Stadium	2006	115%	98%	109%	120%	121%	112%
Kauffman Stadium	2007	103%	90%	104%	127%	117%	101%
Kauffman Stadium	2008	93%	79%	100%	110%	82%	98%
Kauffman Stadium	2009	111%	76%	116%	120%	147%	107%
5 Year Average		104%	84%	106%	118%	111%	104%

Year	Over	Under	Push	Over %	Under %	RF	RA
2005	39	36	6	52%	48%	4.2	6.0
2006	35	43	2	45%	55%	4.2	5.3
2007	41	35	5	54%	46%	5.2	6.2
2008	29	45	7	39%	61%	4.4	4.9
2009	35	46	0	43%	57%	4.2	4.6
	179	205	20	44%	51%	4.4	5.4

ANGEL STADIUM, ANAHEIM

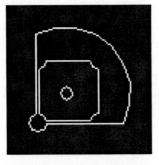

Angel Stadium has undergone several modifications since it was built in 1962. Ground ball pitchers tend to do well here, and teams without a rangy center fielder can struggle covering the outfield. The right field alley is 17 feet closer to home plate than the left field alley. An 18-foot high wall in right field turns many potential home runs into loud doubles, however. The home run rate from left-handed hitters is much lower in this stadium than elsewhere. While run scoring has been higher than league average the last two years, I still consider this a pitcher's park. The under hit 43% of the time in 2009, despite a big jump in the rate of home runs.

PARK NAME	Year	RUNS	HR	H	2B	3B	BB
Angel Stadium	2005	92%	91%	95%	99%	97%	98%
Angel Stadium	2006	91%	80%	103%	94%	79%	96%
Angel Stadium	2007	109%	89%	107%	125%	73%	108%
Angel Stadium	2008	102%	93%	103%	99%	83%	81%
Angel Stadium	2009	102%	122%	100%	93%	61%	97%
5 Year Average		99%	95%	102%	102%	79%	96%

Year	Over	Under	Push	Over %	Under %	RF	RA
2005	36	45	4	44%	56%	4.9	4.1
2006	40	39	4	51%	49%	4.8	4.8
2007	35	41	5	46%	54%	4.5	4.3
2008	41	40	1	51%	49%	5.6	4.4
2009	34	46	3	43%	58%	4.7	4.4
	186	211	17	45%	51%	4.9	4.4

DODGER STADIUM, LOS ANGELES

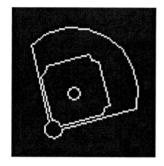

This was known as a pitcher's park, thanks to a large foul ground that helped get pitchers out of jams. That foul territory was reduced in 2006, and scoring increased immediately. That scoring rate has taking a dive over the two years, however. A massive drop in home runs gets the blame. It could be a fluke, or it could be a trend. It bears watching either way. Ground ball pitchers do well here, as do teams with a lot of power bats in their lineup.

PARK NAME	Year	RUNS	HR	H	2B	3B	BB
Dodger Stadium	2005	91%	106%	91%	98%	42%	104%
Dodger Stadium	2006	105%	119%	102%	102%	52%	116%
Dodger Stadium	2007	105%	105%	103%	91%	58%	107%
Dodger Stadium	2008	84%	86%	89%	87%	43%	89%
Dodger Stadium	2009	86%	88%	96%	99%	61%	78%
5 Year Average		94%	101%	96%	95%	51%	99%

Year	Over	Under	Push	Over %	Under %	RF	RA
2005	38	36	7	51%	49%	4.2	5.1
2006	45	35	3	56%	44%	4.4	4.0
2007	50	30	2	63%	38%	5.4	4.6
2008	49	30	2	62%	38%	4.6	4.6
2009	38	44	3	46%	54%	4.3	3.3
	220	175	17	53%	42%	4.6	4.3

MILLER PARK, MILWAUKEE

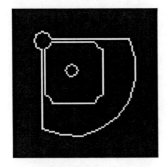

Fly-ball pitchers walk a thin line at Miller Park. Down the lines, the park is deep, but the alleys are short and hitters can take advantage. Foul ball territory is small. The roof keeps the cold out, which hitters appreciate in April and May. Ground ball pitchers do well here. Left-handed hitters see their power numbers suffer while Miller Park helps right-handed power hitters. Run scoring has decreased the last two years, despite the increase in home runs in 2009.

PARK NAME	Year	RUNS	HR	H	2B	3B	BB
Miller Park	2005	100%	109%	90%	88%	96%	104%
Miller Park	2006	100%	101%	95%	98%	136%	110%
Miller Park	2007	101%	112%	94%	105%	50%	110%
Miller Park	2008	95%	89%	96%	86%	138%	113%
Miller Park	2009	89%	107%	93%	107%	109%	100%
5 Year Average		97%	103%	94%	97%	106%	107%

Year	Over	Under	Push	Over %	Under %	RF	RA
2005	35	44	2	44%	56%	4.3	4.5
2006	35	44	2	44%	56%	4.2	4.6
2007	40	37	4	52%	48%	4.8	4.9
2008	48	31	2	61%	39%	5.3	4.5
2009	38	40	5	49%	51%	4.6	4.0
	196	196	15	48%	48%	4.6	4.5

TARGET FIELD, MINNESOTA

Unlike the two New York parks that opened up last year, Minnesota's new ballpark is a major departure from its predecessor. First off: the weather is going to be a huge factor. The average April high temperature in Minneapolis is 55 degrees, not a good way for the offense to rack up high numbers. Minneapolis is also one of the windiest cities in the United States, meaning a bettor needs to pay close attention to which way the wind is blowing before making a wager on the total. Prevailing summer winds coming from the south should push the ball out to right field, helping the left-handed power bats that are in the Twins lineup.

Almost as important as the weather is the difference in size from the Metrodome to Target Field. There is very little foul territory in the new park. This will obviously help out hitters. The distance to the left-field corner is 339 feet, four feet shorter than the old park. The left-center power alley is eight feet shorter, while center is also smaller than the Metrodome. In right field, the distance is the same as the past, including the 26-foot high walls that were in the Metrodome.

NEW YANKEE STADIUM, NEW YORK

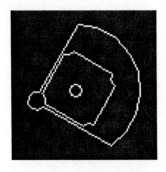

Everything is big in the New Yankee Stadium. The concourses, the seats, the huge Diamond Vision in the outfield, even the Yankee Stadium signs dominate the view. The new stadium opened up with a bang last April; home runs flew out of the place at an alarming rate. Things eventually calmed down. While the home run rate was still much higher, doubles and triples were way down and run scoring was 3% below league average. The early season hype kept the over/under numbers high as well. Over bettors weren't happy; only 44% of the games played in the new stadium went over in 2009. One year park factors are dangerous, so don't get caught up in what is said about the place so far. In 2010, that 44% number could easily be the under rather than the over.

PARK NAME	Year	RUNS	HR	H	2B	3B	BB
Yankee Stadium	2005	140%	143%	162%	123%	182%	122%
Yankee Stadium	2006	88%	102%	96%	101%	38%	94%
Yankee Stadium	2007	99%	118%	102%	99%	69%	86%
Yankee Stadium	2008	104%	98%	98%	100%	105%	100%
New Yankee Stadium	2009	97%	126%	100%	81%	50%	110%
New Park in 2009	2009	97%	126%	100%	81%	50%	110%

Year	Over	Under	Push	Over %	Under %	RF	RA
2005	39	42	3	48%	52%	5.0	5.0
2006	40	43	4	48%	52%	5.4	4.6
2007	35	47	1	43%	57%	5.6	4.4
2008	39	36	8	52%	48%	6.4	4.7
2009	34	43	4	44%	56%	5.1	4.5
	187	211	20	45%	50%	5.5	4.6

CITI FIELD, NEW YORK

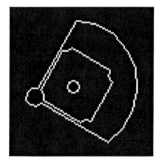

Shea Stadium was always a pitcher's park, and the new stadium for the Mets is no different. I expect the home run rate will decrease in 2010; the large size of the park, weather conditions, sea air, and high walls are bound to come into play. With the drop in home runs will come a drop in runs scored. The Mets went over in 55% of their home games in 2009; I'd be surprised if that was above 50% in 2010.

PARK NAME	Year	RUNS	HR	H	2B	3B	BB
Shea Stadium	2005	97%	89%	101%	95%	71%	101%
Shea Stadium	2006	61%	58%	66%	71%	49%	69%
Shea Stadium	2007	92%	90%	92%	91%	107%	96%
Shea Stadium	2008	95%	108%	93%	94%	50%	109%
Citi Field	2009	94%	106%	96%	96%	120%	94%
New Park in 2009	2009	94%	106%	96%	96%	120%	94%

Year	Over	Under	Push	Over %	Under %	RF	RA
2005	34	43	4	44%	56%	4.4	4.1
2006	40	37	4	52%	48%	4.2	4.4
2007	39	43	5	48%	52%	4.8	4.2
2008	38	40	3	49%	51%	4.5	4.6
2009	41	34	6	55%	45%	4.8	4.3
	192	197	22	47%	48%	4.5	4.3

OAKLAND COLISEUM, OAKLAND

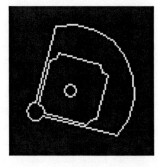 Oakland is a park that plays differently at night than it does during the day. Lower scoring at night, higher scoring during the day. When the weather heats up during the summer, the ball carries well. When it is damp and wet, run scoring decreases. The foul ground is huge and the infield tends to be quick; a team that has speed on defense can do well here. Overall it is a pitcher's park. Right-handers have problems hitting home runs, while lefties have seen some success over the last couple of years. The closing of the 3rd deck prior to the 2006 season may have had an impact. The home run rate fell back to normal after a spike in 2008.

PARK NAME	Year	RUNS	HR	H	2B	3B	BB
Oakland Coliseum	2005	106%	90%	101%	112%	79%	99%
Oakland Coliseum	2006	92%	85%	98%	107%	93%	90%
Oakland Coliseum	2007	83%	79%	87%	79%	126%	106%
Oakland Coliseum	2008	92%	99%	96%	95%	54%	97%
Oakland Coliseum	2009	97%	93%	95%	90%	113%	97%
5 Year Average		94%	89%	95%	97%	93%	98%

Year	Over	Under	Push	Over %	Under %	RF	RA
2005	30	48	3	39%	62%	4.7	3.9
2006	39	40	2	49%	51%	5.0	4.5
2007	39	38	7	51%	49%	4.6	4.3
2008	29	46	6	39%	61%	4.1	4.3
2009	32	42	5	43%	57%	4.0	3.9
	169	214	23	42%	53%	4.5	4.2

CITIZENS BANK PARK, PHILADELPHIA

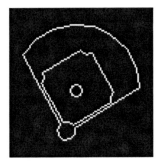

Since opening in 2004, Citizens Bank Park has earned a reputation as one of the best hitting parks in baseball. The visibility seems to be good for hitters; strikeouts are lower compared to the rest of the league. When the weather is hot, the ball flies out of the park. In 2006, the Phillies tried to help its pitchers out by moving the left field fence back five feet. That seems to have helped; the last two seasons have seen home run rates drop after an initial bump in 2007. Runs scored has fallen as well. Right handed power hitters thrive in Citizens Bank.

PARK NAME	Year	RUNS	HR	H	2B	3B	BB
Citizens Bank Park	2005	116%	130%	112%	111%	142%	93%
Citizens Bank Park	2006	106%	120%	101%	103%	65%	96%
Citizens Bank Park	2007	103%	142%	99%	91%	86%	92%
Citizens Bank Park	2008	103%	102%	104%	96%	74%	99%
Citizens Bank Park	2009	103%	101%	102%	105%	90%	102%
5 Year Average		106%	119%	103%	101%	92%	96%

Year	Over	Under	Push	Over %	Under %	RF	RA
2005	35	41	5	46%	54%	4.7	4.1
2006	38	38	5	50%	50%	5.2	4.9
2007	43	36	2	54%	46%	5.5	5.2
2008	41	37	5	53%	47%	5.5	5.2
2009	41	45	2	48%	52%	5.1	4.1
	198	197	19	48%	48%	5.2	4.7

PNC PARK, PITTSBURGH

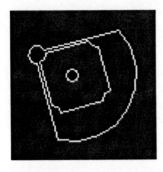

PNC has been flipping between a pitchers park and a run-neutral stadium for a few years now. For now, it is ever so slightly a stadium that favors the pitcher. Fly ball pitchers are helped by the difficulty of hitting home runs in the stadium, particularly out to left field where the dimensions are much bigger than right field. Last year, however, hits that previously fell in for doubles cleared the wall. This was most likely a fluke; expect the home run rate to drop back to normal again in 2010. The infield is a bit rough; a lot of errors are made at PNC compared to other National League parks.

PARK NAME	Year	RUNS	HR	H	2B	3B	BB
PNC Park	2005	103%	87%	106%	113%	132%	101%
PNC Park	2006	101%	82%	112%	126%	100%	98%
PNC Park	2007	95%	78%	100%	108%	58%	88%
PNC Park	2008	90%	87%	102%	106%	93%	98%
PNC Park	2009	102%	105%	105%	94%	71%	97%
5 Year Average		98%	88%	105%	109%	91%	96%

Year	Over	Under	Push	Over %	Under %	RF	RA
2005	34	39	8	47%	53%	4.1	4.7
2006	33	42	5	44%	56%	4.1	4.3
2007	38	40	3	49%	51%	4.7	4.5
2008	36	36	9	50%	50%	4.6	4.8
2009	37	41	3	47%	53%	4.5	5.0
	178	198	28	44%	49%	4.4	4.7

PETCO PARK, SAN DIEGO

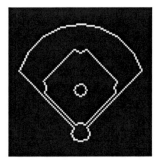 In a perfect world, the prevailing San Diego winds to right field would help hitters overcome the high right field wall at Petco Field. Hitters were also going to be helped by a lower left field wall and smaller foul grounds. Turns out it didn't work out that way. Petco is a pitcher's paradise. Fly-ball pitchers do well there, as do teams with quick outfielders. After a lot of whining from players, the Padres moved in the right center field wall 11 feet before the 2006 season. That helped slightly in 2006, but in 2007 the park went back to the norm. It is still extremely difficult to hit a home run to right field. What Coors Field is for hitters, Petco Park is for pitchers. Remember that when San Diego goes on the road.

PARK NAME	Year	RUNS	HR	H	2B	3B	BB
Petco Park	2005	80%	75%	90%	83%	131%	94%
Petco Park	2006	86%	98%	91%	77%	109%	101%
Petco Park	2007	76%	69%	86%	71%	104%	91%
Petco Park	2008	80%	74%	90%	78%	93%	102%
Petco Park	2009	74%	72%	81%	71%	78%	114%
5 Year Average		79%	78%	87%	76%	103%	101%

Year	Over	Under	Push	Over %	Under %	RF	RA
2005	43	38	2	53%	47%	4.6	5.1
2006	39	39	3	50%	50%	4.1	4.2
2007	36	40	7	47%	53%	3.8	4.1
2008	35	44	2	44%	56%	4.0	3.4
2009	34	45	2	43%	57%	3.6	4.1
	187	206	16	46%	50%	4.0	4.2

SAFECO FIELD, SEATTLE

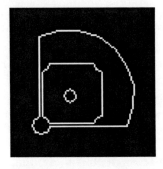

Safeco Field has earned a solid reputation as a fabulous place to pitch. Seattle is located at sea level, and has a dense, humid climate that makes it difficult to hit for a lot of power. The grounds are also huge, particularly to the left field gap where power hitters earn their money. Left-handed hitters have done OK at Safeco the last few years. It is right-handed bats who have struggled. The constant rains may play a role as well. Safeco Field is unique in the fact that the roof only covers the field. The sides are open, allowing wind to play a role even if the roof is "closed". A closed roof may help funnel the western wind out to right field, pushing fly balls to right field out of the park while pushing fly balls to left field toward the deeper center field area. I haven't seen anything other than speculation, but the theory sounds plausible.

PARK NAME	Year	RUNS	HR	H	2B	3B	BB
Safeco Field	2005	97%	84%	102%	97%	60%	104%
Safeco Field	2006	88%	89%	90%	91%	91%	107%
Safeco Field	2007	95%	100%	95%	94%	46%	106%
Safeco Field	2008	93%	90%	99%	92%	122%	102%
Safeco Field	2009	95%	89%	98%	91%	84%	109%
5 Year Average		94%	90%	97%	93%	81%	106%

Year	Over	Under	Push	Over %	Under %	RF	RA
2005	33	41	7	45%	55%	4.3	4.8
2006	40	42	0	49%	51%	3.8	4.7
2007	39	39	3	50%	50%	4.4	4.6
2008	41	37	3	53%	47%	4.7	4.9
2009	42	38	1	53%	48%	4.2	4.7
	195	197	14	48%	49%	4.3	4.7

AT&T PARK, SAN FRANCISCO

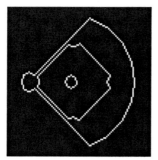 Left-handed power hitters have a horrible time pulling the ball out to right field. While McCovey Cove in right field may be reachable to some, the power alley in right center field is a killer. The deepest part in RCF is 421 away from home plate, cutting the home runs in that part of the field down to half the rate expected from a typical stadium. While home runs are depressed in this park, doubles and triples try to make up for it. The big outfield gaps allow a few more hits to drop in, and keep run scoring in the park near league average. Fly ball pitchers do well here for obvious reasons. Games have tended to go over in recent years.

PARK NAME	Year	RUNS	HR	H	2B	3B	BB
AT&T Park	2005	96%	91%	96%	90%	106%	96%
AT&T Park	2006	99%	68%	97%	108%	105%	99%
AT&T Park	2007	99%	81%	111%	106%	136%	92%
AT&T Park	2008	105%	99%	101%	113%	188%	103%
AT&T Park	2009	105%	97%	101%	102%	111%	86%
5 Year Average		101%	87%	101%	104%	129%	95%

Year	Over	Under	Push	Over %	Under %	RF	RA
2005	33	42	6	44%	56%	4.1	4.6
2006	50	29	3	63%	37%	5.4	5.0
2007	41	37	3	53%	47%	4.7	4.8
2008	31	45	5	41%	59%	4.1	4.5
2009	43	36	2	54%	46%	3.9	5.0
	198	189	19	49%	47%	4.4	4.8

BUSCH STADIUM, ST. LOUIS

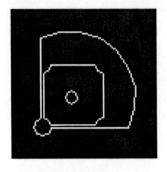

It isn't easy to describe anything costing $346 million as utilitarian, but that's what it is. First opened in 2006, the new Busch Stadium wasn't supposed to play much differently from the old Busch Stadium. For the most part it hasn't. There are better views of the Arch and downtown, and fewer home runs being hit, but the run scoring is down only slightly. Smaller foul grounds seem to even things out for the hitters.

PARK NAME	Year	RUNS	HR	H	2B	3B	BB
Busch Stadium	2005	103%	115%	102%	106%	63%	99%
Busch Stadium	2006	95%	89%	97%	89%	75%	104%
Busch Stadium	2007	93%	72%	103%	97%	104%	96%
Busch Stadium	2008	94%	92%	96%	87%	100%	97%
Busch Stadium	2009	92%	74%	98%	95%	69%	103%
5 Year Average		95%	88%	99%	95%	82%	100%

Year	Over	Under	Push	Over %	Under %	RF	RA
2005	42	42	1	50%	50%	4.9	3.8
2006	37	49	3	43%	57%	5.1	3.9
2007	40	42	6	49%	51%	4.9	4.2
2008	32	41	8	44%	56%	4.5	4.8
2009	36	39	6	48%	52%	4.6	4.4
	187	213	24	44%	50%	4.8	4.2

TROPICANA FIELD, TAMPA BAY

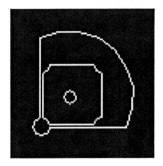

Tropicana Field is one of those ballparks where the less said the better. The turf is incredibly fast and the ball doesn't carry well, so fly ball pitchers with fast outfielders do well here. There are lots of triples here due to the crazy design of the stadium walls. Home runs and doubles are lower than league average. The ballpark has trended towards the under in recent years.

PARK NAME	Year	RUNS	HR	H	2B	3B	BB
Tropicana Field	2005	98%	89%	100%	90%	125%	99%
Tropicana Field	2006	104%	116%	97%	93%	161%	109%
Tropicana Field	2007	89%	96%	94%	91%	100%	95%
Tropicana Field	2008	96%	85%	93%	81%	123%	104%
Tropicana Field	2009	100%	94%	100%	102%	150%	95%
5 Year Average		97%	96%	97%	91%	132%	101%

Year	Over	Under	Push	Over %	Under %	RF	RA
2005	45	32	4	58%	42%	4.4	6.1
2006	34	38	6	47%	53%	4.4	4.7
2007	36	40	5	47%	53%	4.6	5.1
2008	37	38	6	49%	51%	4.6	5.4
2009	41	47	1	47%	53%	4.8	3.7
	193	195	22	47%	48%	4.6	5.0

THE BALLPARK, TEXAS

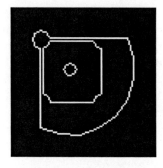

Coors Field East: The Ballpark in Arlington has been one of the best hitting environments in the game. Run scoring took a dive in 2007 but has rebounded back to its normal rate over the last two years. The Ballpark was built with the summer wind in mind. The field is 22 feet below street level. A 42-foot high windscreen was placed on top of the office complex in centerfield in an effort to slow the wind down as well. The engineers may have succeeded too well. The prevailing winds may be stopped out of the southeast, but the winds still come roaring through the concourses towards the field, creating a giant funnel of wind pushing out to center field. Fly-ball pitchers get hammered in the Ballpark. Left-handed hitters love it here.

PARK NAME	Year	RUNS	HR	H	2B	3B	BB
Rangers Ballpark in Arlington	2005	108%	125%	104%	103%	184%	98%
Rangers Ballpark in Arlington	2006	108%	107%	103%	113%	78%	104%
Rangers Ballpark in Arlington	2007	98%	100%	102%	94%	165%	95%
Rangers Ballpark in Arlington	2008	114%	123%	107%	104%	223%	103%
Rangers Ballpark in Arlington	2009	109%	119%	106%	107%	146%	107%
5 Year Average		107%	115%	104%	104%	159%	101%

Year	Over	Under	Push	Over %	Under %	RF	RA
2005	40	38	3	51%	49%	4.9	5.4
2006	38	40	3	49%	51%	6.1	5.1
2007	35	41	5	46%	54%	5.3	5.1
2008	30	46	5	40%	61%	5.2	4.9
2009	41	37	3	53%	47%	6.0	6.3
	184	202	19	45%	50%	5.5	5.4

ROGERS CENTRE, TORONTO

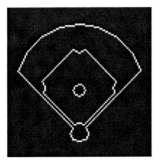

Known as Skydome from its opening in 1989 until 2005, the Rogers Centre was the first park to draw more than four million fans. It is 31 stories high, and was the site of the first World Series game played outside of the United States. Until the 2007 season, Rogers Centre was a hitter's ballpark, especially when the roof is open. When it is closed, the power numbers are slightly down. Fly-ball pitchers do well here. Ground ball pitchers at times struggle, although new field turf was installed in 2006 to replace the older, bouncier fake grass. While power hitters overall are helped by Rogers Centre, righties who can pull the ball thrive here. So do outfielders who can track down fly balls; the deep alleys place a premium on speed in the outfield.

PARK NAME	Year	RUNS	HR	H	2B	3B	BB
Rogers Centre	2005	104%	126%	105%	107%	111%	88%
Rogers Centre	2006	107%	127%	103%	102%	200%	95%
Rogers Centre	2007	94%	116%	91%	106%	118%	94%
Rogers Centre	2008	96%	93%	98%	109%	186%	110%
Rogers Centre	2009	94%	99%	90%	99%	105%	99%
5 Year Average		99%	112%	97%	104%	144%	97%

Year	Over	Under	Push	Over %	Under %	RF	RA
2005	31	46	4	40%	60%	4.6	4.3
2006	36	40	5	47%	53%	4.8	5.3
2007	36	38	7	49%	51%	5.5	4.4
2008	32	49	0	40%	61%	4.7	4.0
2009	34	43	4	44%	56%	4.4	3.6
	169	216	20	42%	53%	4.8	4.3

WASHINGTON NATIONALS

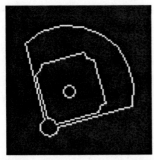

It is tough to get a read on any ballpark with just two years' worth of data, but it looks like the new ball park in Washington plays smaller than the old RFK. Run scoring was up compared to RFK, and while home runs are still down compared to league average, it was now a much more reasonable number. LHers still have a tough time hitting it out; a 14 foot wall in right center field deserves part of the blame. I wouldn't expect to see a lot of high scoring games here. But at least it has become fair to hitters. A few more years' worth of data is needed before drawing any firm conclusions however.

PARK NAME	Year	RUNS	HR	H	2B	3B	BB
RFK Stadium	2005	86%	78%	85%	89%	105%	95%
RFK Stadium	2006	94%	86%	96%	86%	137%	86%
RFK Stadium	2007	87%	68%	96%	106%	81%	93%
Nationals Park	2008	104%	94%	101%	101%	110%	101%
Nationals Park	2009	101%	97%	97%	100%	114%	97%
2 Year Average		102%	96%	99%	101%	112%	99%

Year	Over	Under	Push	Over %	Under %	RF	RA
2005	31	40	10	44%	56%	4.3	4.4
2006	34	44	2	44%	56%	3.6	4.6
2007	41	39	1	51%	49%	4.6	5.1
2008	30	39	12	44%	57%	4.0	4.4
2009	40	38	2	51%	49%	4.0	5.3
	176	200	27	44%	50%	4.1	4.8

MONTH BY MONTH SCORING

It is dangerous to rely on one single number for each team's park factor. Conditions change over the six month baseball season, and the run environment will change as well. The charts below show how each stadium has performed each month of the season over the past 10 years (for most teams). While the sample size still is small (in the 130 game range) and doesn't tell the complete story, it does give a bettor a more detailed clue as to how the conditions will affect scoring.

The table below is ten years' worth of data for the Anaheim Angels. The bigger line is the average number of runs scored in that ballpark during that specific month. An average of 8.91 runs was scored in Anaheim in April from 2000 to 2009. The smaller line is the average runs scored in that month by major league baseball. An average of 9.51 runs was scored in April by all MLB teams. As you can see, run scoring is below average in April, May, June, and September, while above average in July and August.

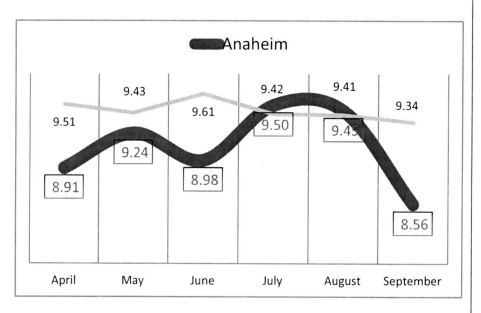

Arizona, Atlanta, and Baltimore

Run scoring dips when the roof is closed in Arizona, leading to a drop in runs once the summer kicks into gear. Atlanta's park plays normal for the summer months but scoring is lower than average in April and September. Baltimore has a surge in July; however, that could be fluky based on the rest of the season.

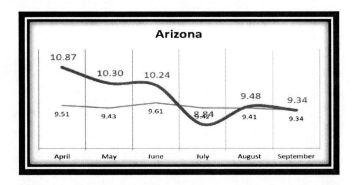

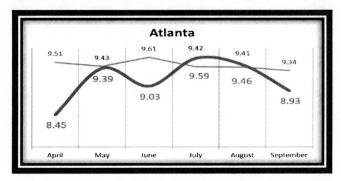

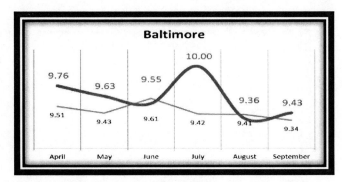

Boston, the Cubs, and the White Sox

The Red Sox scoring takes a spike in August; weather most likely gets the credit. The Cubs scoring fluctuates all season, usually depending on the direction of the wind. As the weather heats up, so does scoring in Cellular One Ballpark. The home run rate increases dramatically as the season turns into summer.

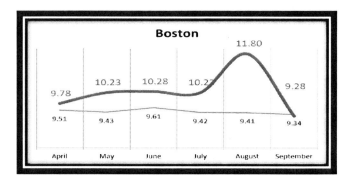

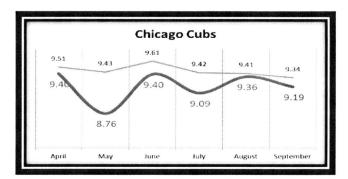

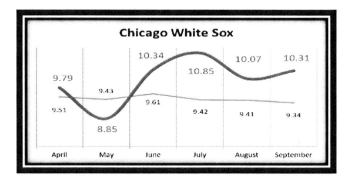

Cincinnati, Cleveland, and Colorado

The Reds ballpark historically has helped out hitters, regardless of the weather conditions. While scoring gradually increases into the summer months, it isn't out of the ordinary. The Indians see a large spike in run production as spring turns into summer. Colorado does have some weather problems early and late in the season, but they do not seem to affect scoring on a macro level.

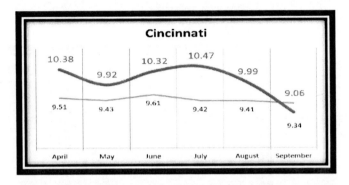

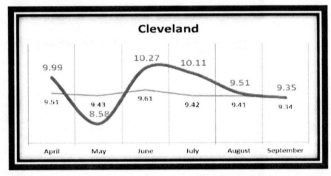

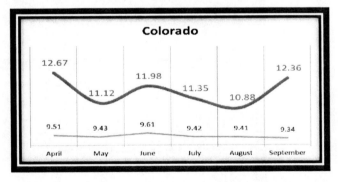

Detroit, Florida, and Houston

Detroit plays at league average for most of the season, with the exception being May. The Marlins have one of the better pitcher's parks in baseball until the scoring increases in September. I'm not sure the reasons for this; Miami weather in September isn't too different from its weather in August. The bats start out quick in Houston, but scoring takes a dive as the season gets going and stays there the rest of the way. Air conditioning probably deserves most of the blame.

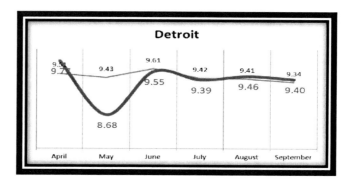

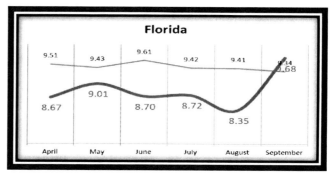

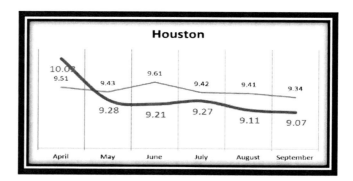

Kansas City, Los Angeles, and Milwaukee

The Royals scoring seems to follow along with the weather: the hotter it is, the more runs scored. Wind may play a bigger role as well. Los Angeles remains steady, other than a short blip in July. Other factors probably come into play. Milwaukee doesn't deal with cold or otherwise bad weather. If it is uncomfortable outside, the roof will close.

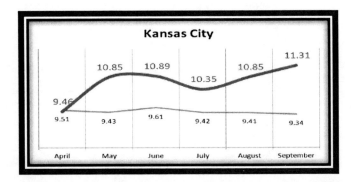

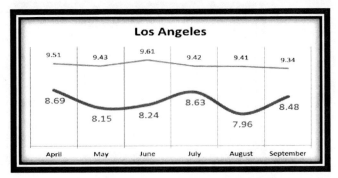

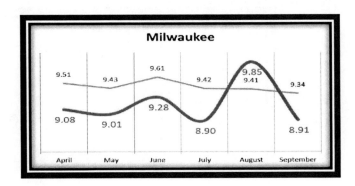

Minnesota, the Yankees, and the Mets

An indoor stadium means that any change in scoring over the course of the season has nothing to do with the weather. That will change as the Twins move to a new ballpark this year. The data listed below for both New York teams doesn't count the 2009 season. The Yankees see a scoring spike that follows the temperature trend. Scoring for the Mets is relatively steady other than the extremes in April and September.

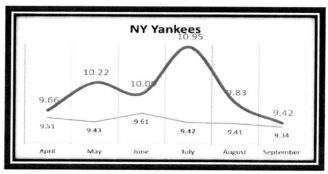

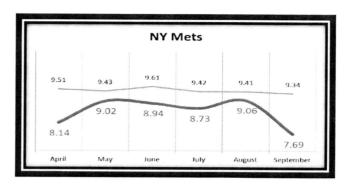

Oakland, Philadelphia, and Pittsburgh

Oakland is a rare stadium in that scoring goes down as the summer heats up. Wind conditions or the increased number of night games compared to the rest of the year may play a role. Philadelphia peaks in June and bottoms out in August. Pittsburgh is the opposite, peaking in August while bottoming out in June. I don't take much stock into either of those fluctuations.

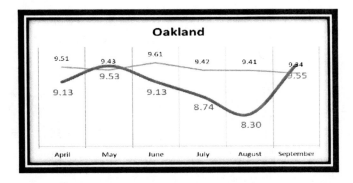

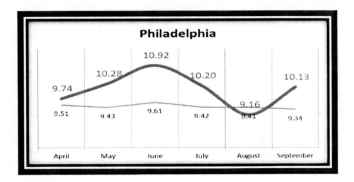

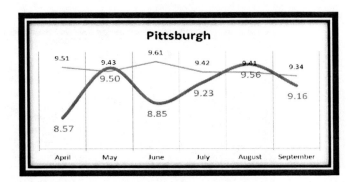

The Padres' ballpark looks steady other than the July bump. Seattle is steady as well, most likely due to its roof that will keep bad weather out. The increase in July and August might be due to the roof being open. The Giants' location next to the bay means factors other than game time temperature play a bigger role in scoring.

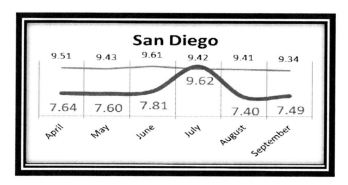

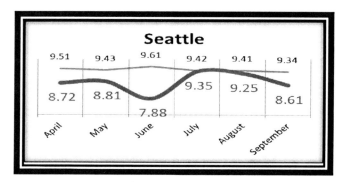

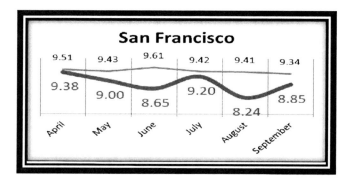

St. Louis, Tampa Bay, Texas

The Cardinals see an increase in runs in June and July, but that dips back down as the weather cools. Tampa plays every home game inside, so any change in the scoring rate is due to something other than weather. Texas plays in one of the highest scoring parks in the country, due in no small part because of the temperature and wind effects. Pay particular attention to the wind.

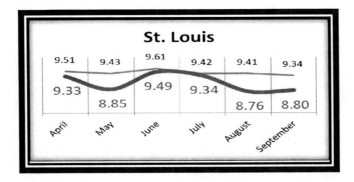

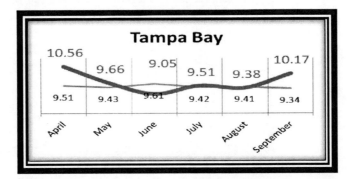

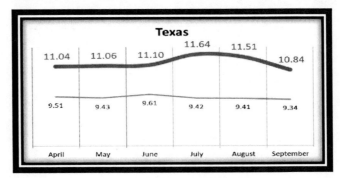

Toronto, and Washington

The Blue Jays close the roof when the weather is poor, so fluctuations in scoring aren't from the weather. Washington has only played several years in their new ballpark so it is impossible to get a good read on how it will play at different times in the year.

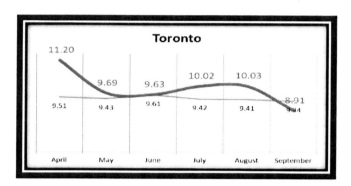

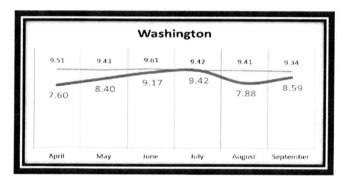

THE STRIKE ZONE

The rulebook defines the strike zone as "that area over home plate which is a horizontal line at the midpoint between the top of the shoulders and the top of the uniform pants, and the lower level is a line at the top of the knees. The strike zone shall be determined from the batter's stance as the batter is prepared to swing."

In theory, the strike zone seems simple. In actuality however, it is a judgment call from the home plate umpire. Each batter's strike zone is different from the next, depending on a batter's position when he is swinging the bat. Jimmy Rollins's strike zone is smaller than Richie Sexson's because Rollins is A) 5 feet 9 inches tall compared to Sexson's height of 6 feet 4 inches, and B) Sexson stands high when he's in the box while Rollins tends to crouch.

This is a discrepancy acknowledged by everyone involved in the game. According to most players, a good umpire is one whose strike zone is consistent from one player's first at-bat to his next. If, however, the high strike is called a ball in the first inning but a strike in the fifth, then the players will have a problem.

Today's strike zone has evolved into a box more than the rectangle dictated in the rulebooks. The high strike simply isn't called much anymore.

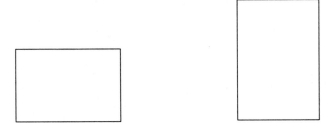

Current Strike Zone   True Strike Zone

MLB would prefer a standardize strike zone, and have taken some steps to encourage this. Computer technology was brought into baseball when MLB became concerned about length of the game and the inconsistency of the home plate umpire. First Ques-tec, now Pitch Fx. Both systems use cameras and tracking devices to help determine whether a pitch was called correctly by an umpire.

Over the course of a game, an umpire might miss up to a dozen pitches (according to Pitch Fx). Consistent umpires will tend to miss the same type of pitchers, giving savvy gamblers a betting opportunity. A pitcher's umpire will go 'under'; a hitter's umpire will tend to go 'over'.

The size of the strike zone is the key. Obviously the more walks in the game the more runs will be scored. But walks don't tell the whole story. Assume that the pitcher just threw a 2-1 pitch on the outside corner of the plate. A pitcher's umpire will call that strike two. The hitter's umpire will make the count 3-1. It is impossible to minimize the importance of the 2-1 pitch. In 2003 the New York Yankees, with a 2-2 count, had a .339 slugging percentage. With a 3-1 count, the Yankees had a .694 slugging percentage. That call on the corner, depending on which way it went, either turned the average Yankee hitter into a Brent Mayne (.344 slug % in 2003) or an Albert Pujols (.667 slug % in 2003).

An umpire sees hundreds of thousands of pitches throughout his career. He already has his strike zone defined by the time he reaches the major leagues, and as such will tend to keep calling balls and strikes the way he always has. A pitcher's umpire will likely remain one until he retires. The same holds true for a hitter's umpire. A successful gambler must know which is which. He must know what way that 2-1 pitches will likely go. Failure to keep detailed, accurate records will mean failure to maximize your profits over the course of the baseball season.

THE UMPIRE ROTATION

Umpires typically move clockwise from game to game. The 3rd base ump moves to 2nd base, 2nd moves to 1st, 1st base goes to home, and the home umpire moves over to 3rd after he calls balls and strikes. The introduction of umpire vacations, however, has caused some changes in this movement. AAA umpires rarely umpire games behind home plate. MLB also takes advantage of doubleheaders to give umpires additional rest; an AAA umpire is often called up to work these games. In Game 1, the AAA umpire usually starts at 3rd base, then moves over to 1st base for the nightcap. The Game 2 home plate umpire usually doesn't work the first game. The home plate umpire in the first game of the double header also gets a game off. When dealing with doubleheaders, a bettor needs to be on his toes.

ADJUSTING YOUR TOTALS

Bob McCune, in his book "Insights into Sports Betting", advises adjusting your projected total downward by ½ run when a pitcher's umpire is behind the plate. He defines such as a home plate umpire that goes under in 60% or more of his games. When an umpire goes under 70% or more, McCune would take a full run off his expected total for the game. The opposite is true as well. I have found these adjustments an effective way to account for the home plate umpire in most instances. Many bettors will blindly bet the under when a pitcher's umpire is calling balls and strikes. This is a very big mistake and should obviously be avoided. The sports books know who is going to umpire home plate; they will adjust the total if they feel it is necessary. A gambler must make his own total line, tweak it according to the umpire, and only then make a play based on those numbers.

HOMER UMPIRES

Just as there are 'Over' umpires, there are also homer umpires. Homer umpires tend to take the path of least resistance; consciously or subconsciously, the umpire will go with the crowd and tends to call the borderline pitches for the home team. There are also umpires that will go the other way. Some enjoy being the most hated man in the ballpark, and will tend to call the close ones against the home team. Keeping accurate records again will alert you to these umpires; understand, however, that statistical flukes may account for these types of umpires.

Umpires all have their little quirks when they umpire games. Some umpires favor veterans; Bruce Froemming was one of these. Young players couldn't stand him for this. Others, when faced with a meaningless game in the middle of August, will go through the motions and try to get the ballgame over as quickly as possible. Some umpires will try to avoid calling a third strike; others, when a borderline pitch is thrown, will let the count affect what the call will do. If the count is 2-1, the close pitch is a strike. If the count is 1-2, the close pitch will be a ball.

Some umpires will widen the strike zone when it is hot out. A few will do so when it is cold. Some umpires will call the high curve ball for a strike. Steve Palermo, one of the best umpires in the game before he was paralyzed breaking up a robbery, would reward a pitcher who showed guts in throwing a high curve ball. The opposite is true as well. Many umpires will quit on the high curve ball and not give that pitch to a pitcher. David Wells and Barry Zito certainly know which umpires give them the high strike; a bettor should know as well.

OVER/UNDER UMPIRES

Based on the last five years' worth of games, the following umpires have shown a tendency to call high scoring games or low scoring games. The hard data only tells part of the story. It is important to watch an umpire call balls and strikes for a few games before making a judgment on that umpire's strike zone. And remember, the umpire should be a secondary aspect when you handicap.

Under Umpires	Over Umpires
Ted Barrett	Jerry Crawford
Mark Carlson	Gerry Davis
Fieldin Culbreth	Laz Diaz
Mike Estabrook	Chad Fairchild
Andy Fletcher	Sam Holbrooke
Marty Foster	Marvin Hudson
Ron Kulpa	Tim McClelland
Bill Miller	Ed Montegue
Brian O'Nora	Mike Reilly
Brian Runge	Jim Reynolds
Dale Scott	Paul Schrieber
Mike Winters	Tim Timmons
Jim Wolf	Tim Tschida

UMPIRE ROSTER

LANCE BARKSDALE

Full name Robert Lance Barksdale
Born March 8, 1967, Brookhaven, Mississippi
Umpired First Game: May 29, 2000
Height: 5' 10" Weight: 175
Ejections: 2000 (2), 2001 (2), 2002 (4), 2003 (4), 2004 (6), 2005 (3), 2006 (1),
2007 (4), 2008 (3), 2009 (3).
Total: 32

Barksdale will be entering his fourth complete season as a full-time major league umpire in 2010. He was one of the more experienced rookie umpires; he had been a vacation fill-in for major league baseball since the 2000 season. He'll turn 43 this March. Barksdale had his name put into the record books by being the first umpire ever to have a home run call reversed by instant replay. An Adam LaRoche drive, initially ruled a homer by Barksdale, was ruled a double after the umpires got a second look at it on reply. His strike zone tends to be on the smaller side but that doesn't translate into an Over umpire.

Year	Over	Under	%	Runs/Gm	Strike %
2004	14	10	58%	10.5	62.7%
2005	13	23	36%	7.7	63.0%
2006	12	13	48%	9.6	62.6%
2007	17	16	52%	9.6	62.0%
2008	14	15	48%	8.9	61.9%
2009	17	17	50%	9.5	61.8%
TOTAL	87	94	48%	9.3	62.3%

Year	H Win	H Lose	Win%	Home R/G	Road R/G
2004	13	11	54.2	5.4	5.1
2005	22	15	59.5	4.2	3.5
2006	14	15	48.3	4.3	5.3
2007	22	13	62.9	5.1	4.5
2008	20	14	59.2	4.7	4.2
TOTAL	91	68	58%	4.7	4.5

TED BARRETT

Full name Edward George Barrett
Born July 31, 1965, Pasco, Washington
Umpired First Game: May 28, 1994
Height: 6' 4" Weight: 255
Ejections: 1994 (2), 1996 (5), 1997 (3), 1998 (2), 1999 (2), 2000 (1), 2001 (6),
2002 (6), 2003 (3), 2004 (2), 2005 (9), 2006 (3), 2007 (2), 2008 (2), 2009 (2).
Total: 50

Not many umpires can say they sparred with Evander Holyfield and Greg Page, but Ted Barrett has that on his resume. A graduate from Cal State Hayward with a B.S. in Kinesiology, Barrett was an outstanding amateur boxer. His father wanted to keep him out of the ring and paid Barrett's way to Joe Brinkman's umpiring school. After Barrett finished at the top of the class, he took a job with the Northwest League and made a rapid rise through the ranks. Barrett quickly has become one of the best umpires in the game. He maintains control of the game, has a consistent (if generous) strike zone and is very well respected throughout the game. His games have trended towards the Under in recent years.

Year	Over	Under	%	Runs/Gm	Strike %
2004	14	18	44%	9.7	63.0%
2005	18	14	56%	9.3	69.1%
2006	16	19	46%	9.5	63.6%
2007	14	16	47%	10.1	62.9%
2008	16	18	47%	8.2	62.9%
2009	13	21	38%	8.3	62.6%
TOTAL	91	106	46%	9.2	64.0%

Year	H Win	H Lose	Win%	Home R/G	Road R/G
2004	14	19	42%	4.3	5.4
2005	19	15	56%	4.7	4.6
2006	25	10	71%	5.6	4
2007	14	20	41%	4.7	5.4
2008	21	13	62%	4.6	3.7
2009	23	11	68%	4.5	4.1
TOTAL	116	88	57%	5.6	5.4

SCOTT BARRY

Full name Scott Adam Barry
Born August 3, 1976, Battle Creek, Michigan
Umpired First Game: June 4, 2006
Height: 5' 11" Weight: 195
Ejections: 2007 (1)

Barry is a 33 year old AAA umpire who spent last season as a vacation fill-in at the major league level. He began umpiring in 2000 in the Gulf Coast League and has quickly worked his way up through the Appalachian League, Midwest League, the World Baseball Classic, the Eastern League and International League. My notes indicate he has typical strike zone for umpires: a little wide on the corners and tight on the high/low pitches. His accuracy isn't the greatest, typical for an inexperienced umpire.

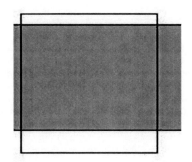

Year	Over	Under	%	Runs/Gm	Strike %
2006	1	4	20%	7.6	63.3%
2007	7	1	88%	12.2	59.1%
2008	14	16	47%	9.9	62.8%
2009	14	24	37%	8.5	61.3%
TOTAL	36	45	44%	9.55	61.6%

Year	H Win	H Lose	Win%	Home R/G	Road R/G
2006	4	1	80%	4	3.6
2007	4	4	50%	6.4	5.9
2008	18	12	60%	6	3.9
2009	18	21	46%	4.4	4.2
TOTAL	**44**	**38**	**54%**	**6.4**	**5.9**

WALLY BELL

Full name Wallace Robert Bell
Born January 10, 1965, Ravenna, Ohio
Umpired First Game: June 16, 1992
Height: 6' 2" Weight: 240
Ejections: 1994 (5), 1995 (1), 1996 (3), 1997 (4), 1998 (4), 1999 (2), 2000 (2),
2001 (2), 2002 (5), 2003 (1), 2004 (2), 2006 (2), 2007 (1), 2008 (4).
Total: 38

Bell is confrontational to both players and managers, and often goes out of his way to escalate tensions when he believes a player is showing him up. Bell has a large, inconsistent strike zone; one never knows what one will get when he is behind the plate. Overall, he tends to help pitchers with his large strike zone. Pitchers who work the corners are helped by Bell; his zone tends to be more horizontal than most. On a day-to-day basis, it is best to expect the unexpected. Bell has umpired in the major leagues since 1993.

Year	Over	Under	%	Runs/Gm	Strike %
2004	18	15	55%	10.5	63.7%
2005	15	18	45%	8.8	63.3%
2006	18	14	56%	10	63.1%
2007	17	15	53%	10	63.2%
2008	11	19	37%	9.1	63.0%
2009	16	18	47%	9.4	62.7%
TOTAL	95	99	49%	9.63	63.2%

Year	H Win	H Lose	Win%	Home R/G	Road R/G
2004	15	19	44%	5.0	5.5
2005	24	10	71%	5.1	3.7
2006	24	11	69%	5.4	4.6
2007	17	16	52%	4.9	5.1
2008	24	12	67%	5.1	4.1
2009	25	13	66%	5.0	4.2
TOTAL	129	81	61%	5.4	5.3

C.B. BUCKNOR

Full name CB Bucknor
Born August 23, 1962, Savanna la Mar, Jamaica
Umpired First Game: April 4, 1996
Height: 6' 2" Weight: 215
Ejections: 1999 (1), 2000 (1), 2001 (2), 2002 (2), 2003 (2), 2004 (2), 2005 (4),
2006 (2), 2007 (1).
Total: 17

Sometimes you can't turn your head. This goes for car wrecks, fine sunsets, and any game that has C.B. Bucknor behind the plate. When Bucknor is calling a game, you know something interesting is going to happen. It could be C.B.'s atrocious work calling strikes, his awful attitude, or just the general cloud that perpetually hangs over C.B.'s head everywhere he goes. If ESPN shows a manager losing his cool, assume Bucknor was the cause. It isn't enough to blow a call; C.B. tends to twist the knife with a smile on his face. One of Lou Piniella's most famous tantrums was the result of Bucknor's smirk that set Sweet Lou off. Another classic argument came about when C.B. refused to call time out so Dan Wheeler could keep the ball after getting his first major league hit. Bucknor has been a major league umpire since 1999. He was born in Jamaica and moved to the United States when he was 11 years old. He had been an Over umpire prior to the 2008 season but that has changed over the last two years.

Year	Over	Under	%	Runs/Gm	Strike %
2004	21	9	70%	11.3	62.1%
2005	18	16	53%	10.3	63.3%
2006	19	15	56%	10.1	62.5%
2007	17	13	57%	9.9	61.9%
2008	11	19	37%	8.4	63.0%
2009	17	18	49%	9.1	62.1%
TOTAL	103	90	53%	9.85	62.5%

Year	H Win	H Lose	Win%	Home R/G	Road R/G
2004	20	15	57%	5.3	6.0
2005	16	18	47%	4.9	5.3
2006	20	14	59%	5.5	4.6
2007	20	14	59%	5.4	4.5
2008	21	12	64%	4.6	3.8
2009	21	14	60%	5.1	4.1
TOTAL	118	87	58%	5.5	5.0

ANGEL CAMPOS

Full name Angel Hernandez Campos
Born August 22, 1973, Montclair, California
Umpired First Game: May 3, 2007
Height: 5' 9" Weight: 190

Campos has been a vacation umpire at the major league level the last three seasons. He's 36 years old and officially works in the Pacific League. Campos seems to have a small strike zone; he doesn't like giving out low strikes in the games I saw. The Over hit just 41% of his games in 2009, a big change from 2008 (77% Over).

Year	Over	Under	%	Runs/Gm	Strike
2007	2	3	40%	9.8	63.3%
2008	17	5	77%	11.3	63.0%
2009	11	16	41%	8.9	63.1%
TOTAL	30	24	56%	10	63.1%

Year	H Win	H Lose	Win%	Home R/G	Road R/G
2007	2	4	33%	4.3	5.5
2008	9	15	38%	5.2	6.1
2009	16	11	59%	4.6	4.3
TOTAL	27	30	47%	4.5	4.6

MARK CARLSON

Full name Mark Christopher Carlson
Born July 11, 1969, Joliet, Illinois
Umpired First Game: June 11, 1999
Height: 6' 0" Weight: 210
Ejections: 2000 (4), 2001 (1), 2002 (3), 2003 (11), 2004 (4), 2005 (2), 2006 (1),
2007 (4), 2009 (3)
Total: 33

Carlson is a solid umpire, although his strike zone is inconsistent small at times. Carlson began umpiring after leaving the Marine Corps in 1993. He moved through the ranks quickly and became a fulltime major league umpire in 1999. A former catcher in college, Carlson played with former big leaguer Steve Parris at Joliet West high school. Parris's numbers in two starts with Carlson as home plate umpire? 15 innings pitched, one earned run, two walks, and 12 strikeouts.

Year	Over	Under	%	Runs/Gm	Strike
2004	13	22	37%	8.9	62.0%
2005	14	21	40%	8	62.5%
2006	15	17	47%	9.1	63.2%
2007	14	20	41%	8.9	62.9%
2008	0	1	0%	5	57.6%
2009	12	21	36%	8.1	63.0%
TOTAL	68	102	40%	8	61.9%

Year	H Win	H Lose	Win%	Home R/G	Road R/G
2004	18	17	51%	4.3	4.6
2005	18	17	51%	4.4	3.6
2006	22	10	69%	5.2	3.9
2007	17	17	50%	4.5	4.4
2008	1	0	100%	4.0	1.0
2009	22	12	65%	4.1	3.9
TOTAL	98	73	57%	5.2	4.6

GARY CEDERSTROM

Full name Gary L. Cederstrom
Born October 4, 1955, Bismark, North Dakota
Umpired First Game: June 2, 1989
Height: 6' 3" Weight: 250
Ejections: 1990 (2), 1991 (1), 1995 (2), 1996 (1), 1997 (1), 1998 (3), 1999 (6),
2001 (3), 2002 (3), 2003 (2), 2004 (4), 2005 (1), 2007 (1).
Total: 30

Cederstrom is a 53-year-old umpire that spends his off-season living in Minot, North Dakota, a town near the Canadian border 105 miles north of Bismarck. Cederstrom has been a full time major league umpire since 1997. He seems to have a small strike zone but that hasn't translated into an over tendency. Cederstrom is consistent with his zone and handles in-game situations very well.

Year	Over	Under	%	Runs/Gm	Strike
2004	20	14	59%	10.7	62.2%
2005	16	17	48%	9.9	63.0%
2006	18	12	60%	10.5	62.2%
2007	16	16	50%	9.3	63.5%
2008	16	18	47%	8.5	63.0%
2009	13	16	45%	8.7	63.1%
TOTAL	99	93	52%	9.6	62.8%

Year	H Win	H Lose	Win%	Home R/G	Road R/G
2004	24	11	69%	5.9	4.8
2005	22	12	65%	5.3	4.6
2006	19	13	59%	5.3	5.2
2007	20	13	61%	4.9	4.5
2008	21	14	60%	4.7	3.8
2009	24	8	75%	5.0	3.7
TOTAL	130	71	65%	5.9	5.2

ERIC COOPER

Full name Eric Richard Cooper
Born December 18, 1966, Des Moines, Iowa
Umpired First Game: June 17, 1996
Height: 5' 10" Weight: 215
Ejections: 1996 (1), 1997 (1), 1998 (2), 1999 (5), 2000 (4), 2001 (7), 2002 (1),
2003 (6), 2004 (2), 2005 (5), 2006 (4), 2007 (1), 2008 (6), 2009 (7).
Total: 52

Cooper first became a full-time major league umpire in 1999. A graduate of Iowa State University, Cooper has earned a reputation as a hothead with a quick trigger. Cooper made the news in 2004 with his baiting and ejection of Kerry Wood in April, 2004. In the past, he has bumped Bob Brenly during an argument and given Wade Boggs the first ejection in his 17-year career after Boggs argued a strike call. Cooper has an inconsistent strike zone and a bad attitude to go along with it. Born in Des Moines, Cooper graduated from Iowa State with a major in transportation logistics.

Year	Over	Under	%	Runs/Gm	Strike
2004	17	18	49%	9.8	61.7%
2005	15	19	44%	9.5	63.2%
2006	17	16	52%	9.6	62.8%
2007	16	13	55%	9.6	63.4%
2008	15	15	50%	9.7	63.4%
2009	18	14	56%	9.8	63.4%
TOTAL	98	95	51%	9.7	63.0%

Year	H Win	H Lose	Win%	Home R/G	Road R/G
2004	13	24	35%	4.4	5.3
2005	19	16	54%	5.0	4.5
2006	18	16	53%	5.0	4.6
2007	17	15	53%	5.1	4.5
2008	19	14	58%	5.2	4.5
2009	17	14	55%	5.0	4.7
TOTAL	103	99	51%	5.3	5.2

DERRYL COUSINS

Full name Derryl Cousins
Born August 18, 1946, Fresno, California
Umpired First Game: April 6, 1979
Height: 6' 0" Weight: 205
Ejections: 1979 (7), 1980 (4), 1981 (1), 1982 (1), 1983 (6), 1984 (2), 1985 (10), 1986 (10), 1987 (9), 1988 (2), 1989 (1), 1990 (6), 1991 (2), 1992 (2), 1993 (4), 1995 (4), 1996 (1), 1997 (4), 1998 (2), 1999 (3), 2000 (5), 2001 (3), 2002 (3), 2003 (5), 2004 (1), 2005 (2), 2007 (3), 2008 (4).
Total: 107

Cousins was hired as a replacement umpire during the 1979 umpire strike. Thought by many of his fellow umpire to be a scab, he was not allowed to join the former umpire union run by Richie Phillips. He is, however, a member of the new MLB umpires union that replaced the Major League Umpires Association. Cousins played pro ball in the Detroit and Cleveland organizations from 1966-1972. His strike zone tends to be large…he will call the high strike.

Year	Over	Under	%	Runs/Gm	Strike
2004	6	12	33%	9.2	61.7%
2005	13	17	43%	9.2	61.1%
2006	21	13	62%	10.7	62.5%
2007	13	16	45%	9	62.4%
2008	17	18	49%	9.2	62.1%
2009	15	18	45%	8.8	61.5%
TOTAL	85	94	47%	9.4	61.9%

Year	H Win	H Lose	Win%	Home R/G	Road R/G
2004	7	11	39%	4.2	4.9
2005	21	12	64%	4.6	4.6
2006	19	16	54%	5.5	5.1
2007	17	16	52%	4.8	4.2
2008	25	10	71%	5.0	4.2
2009	21	13	62%	4.6	4.1
TOTAL	110	78	59%	5.5	5.1

JERRY CRAWFORD

Full name Gerald Joseph Crawford
Born August 13, 1947, Philadelphia, Pennsylvania
Umpired First Game: May 15, 1976
Height: 5' 11" Weight: 185
Son of Shag Crawford
Ejections: 1977 (3), 1978 (4), 1979 (5), 1980 (7), 1984 (1), 1986 (1), 1987 (3),
1988 (1), 1989 (3), 1990 (4), 1991 (2), 1992 (6), 1993 (6), 1994 (1), 1996 (3), 1998
(3), 1999 (2), 2000 (7), 2001 (1), 2002 (6), 2003 (5), 2004 (1), 2007 (1).
Total: 76

Crawford has umpiring in his blood; his father Henry was a major league umpire for 20 years before retiring in 1975. His brother, Joe, is a well-known referee in the NBA. One of the best umpires in the game, Crawford is thought by many to have the most consistent strike zone in baseball. Be careful when he umpires the Cardinals; Tony LaRussa and Crawford have had a long running feud that LaRussa believes affects Crawford's calls during games.

Year	Over	Under	%	Runs/Gm	Strike
2004	16	13	55%	10.1	61.6%
2005	16	10	62%	9.9	63.5%
2006	19	12	61%	12.3	61.0%
2007	7	8	47%	10.2	61.5%
2008	12	9	57%	11.4	60.8%
2009	12	12	50%	10.4	60.5%
TOTAL	82	64	56%	10.7	61.5%

Year	H Win	H Lose	Win%	Home R/G	Road R/G
2004	15	14	52%	5.0	5.1
2005	12	15	44%	4.7	5.1
2006	18	15	55%	6.5	5.8
2007	8	8	50%	5.6	4.6
2008	9	15	38%	5.3	6.1
2009	18	7	72%	6.2	4.2
TOTAL	80	74	52%	5.2	5.5

FIELDIN CULBRETH

Full name Fieldin Henry Culbreth
Born March 16, 1963, Spartanburg, South Carolina
Umpired First Game: August 13, 1993
Height: 5' 11" Weight: 225
Ejections: 1994 (2), 1995 (1), 1996 (2), 1997 (6), 1998 (1), 2000 (2), 2001 (2),
2002 (1), 2003 (5), 2004 (1), 2005 (3), 2006 (2), 2008 (2).
Total: 30

Culbreth has been a major league umpire since 1999. As a pitcher/right fielder at North Carolina Charlotte, Culbreth played with former Angel/Marlin Bryan Harvey and was named to the Sunbelt All-Conference team. An arm injury pushed him into umpiring. Culbreth has shown himself to be a pitcher's umpire, with a rather inconsistent strike zone. He is a pretty solid umpire whose games tend to lean toward the Under.

Year	Over	Under	%	Runs/Gm	Strike
2004	15	17	47%	9.5	62.6%
2005	14	19	42%	9.4	63.1%
2006	20	11	65%	10.5	62.5%
2007	15	19	44%	9.4	62.7%
2008	16	17	48%	8.8	62.2%
2009	14	19	42%	8.7	61.8%
TOTAL	94	102	48%	9.4	62.5%

Year	H Win	H Lose	Win%	Home R/G	Road R/G
2004	17	15	53%	5.0	4.5
2005	16	19	46%	4.3	5.1
2006	22	11	67%	5.9	4.6
2007	20	14	59%	5.2	4.2
2008	12	22	35%	3.9	4.9
2009	20	14	59%	4.4	4.3
TOTAL	107	95	53%	4.8	4.6

PHIL CUZZI

Full name Philip Cuzzi
Born August 29, 1955, Newark, New Jersey
Umpired First Game: June 4, 1991
Height: 5' 10" Weight: 200
Ejections: 1993 (4), 1999 (4), 2000 (4), 2001 (4), 2002 (6), 2003 (12), 2004 (4),
2005 (7), 2007 (10), 2008 (1). Total: 56

Cuzzi brought his act to the national stage in the 2005 NL Championship Series. His erratic strike zone was a site to behold, topped off by his ejection of Jim Edmonds and Tony LaRussa in the late stages of Game 4. Don't look for him anytime soon in a playoff game. Cuzzi has been in the major leagues since 1999, and is one of the more arrogant and confrontational umpires in the game. He is not a good umpire, and shows poor judgment in all phases of the game. Will usually call the high strike; from what I've seen most pitches that cross the plate will be strikes regardless of height.

Year	Over	Under	%	Runs/Gm	Strike
2004	15	20	43%	9.2	63.6%
2005	17	14	55%	9	63.2%
2006	14	20	41%	8.9	63.9%
2007	19	14	58%	10.2	63.1%
2008	15	16	48%	8.5	64.1%
2009	12	22	35%	8.7	63.3%
TOTAL	92	106	46%	9.1	63.5%

Year	H Win	H Lose	Win%	Home R/G	Road R/G
2004	18	18	50%	4.3	5.0
2005	21	14	60%	4.8	4.2
2006	16	19	46%	4.5	4.4
2007	22	13	63%	6.1	4.1
2008	21	12	64%	4.6	3.9
2009	20	14	59%	4.6	4.1
TOTAL	118	90	57%	4.7	4.4

KERWIN DANLEY

Full name Kerwin Joseph Danley
Born May 25, 1961, Los Angeles, California
Umpired First Game: June 12, 1992
Height: 6' 2" Weight: 240
Ejections: 1993 (3), 1998 (4), 1999 (2), 2000 (3), 2001 (5), 2002 (7), 2003 (4),
2004 (2), 2005 (1), 2008 (1), 2009 (0). Total: 32

Danley has been calling major league baseball games since 1998. A 1983 first team All-American out of San Diego State, Danley played college baseball with Tony Gwynn, Bobby Meachem, Mark Grace and Al Newman. He has a large strike zone and tends to be a pitcher's umpire. Danley missed much of the 2009 season after getting hit with the barrel of a bat while umpiring home plate. That was the second season in a row Danley has been injured on the field. In 2008, he was stuck on the jaw by a Brad Penny pitch and missed six weeks of the season.

Year	Over	Under	%	Runs/Gm	Strike
2004	14	17	45%	9.4	61.6%
2005	12	9	57%	9.3	62.8%
2006	17	17	50%	9.9	62.7%
2007	16	16	50%	9.5	63.0%
2008	11	15	42%	8.5	61.9%
2009	5	4	56%	9.6	61.7%
TOTAL	75	78	49%	9.4	62.3%

Year	H Win	H Lose	Win%	Home R/G	Road R/G
2004	17	16	52%	4.8	4.6
2005	11	10	52%	4.8	4.5
2006	18	16	53%	5.2	4.7
2007	15	19	44%	4.3	5.2
2008	16	10	62%	4.6	3.9
2009	3	7	30%	4.0	5.6
TOTAL	80	78	51%	4.9	4.5

GARY DARLING

Full name Gary Richard Darling
Born October 9, 1957, San Francisco, California
Umpired First Game: June 3, 1986
Height: 6' 3" Weight: 215
Ejections: 1986 (2), 1987 (8), 1988 (4), 1989 (6), 1990 (4), 1991 (10), 1992 (15),
1993 (5), 1995 (2), 1996 (5), 1997 (3), 1998 (4), 1999 (5), 2002 (3), 2003 (2), 2004
(3), 2005 (4), 2006 (2), 2007 (1), 2008 (1), 2009 (3).
Total: 92

Darling began umpiring in the major leagues in 1988. He lost his job in the Richie Phillips negotiation fiasco, but was reinstated in 2002 as a partial settlement due to a lawsuit filed against MLB. He is a temperamental umpire who gets involved in more than his fair share of arguments, and is a poor home plate umpire regarding balls/strikes call. He loves calling the high strikes.

Year	Over	Under	%	Runs/Gm	Strike
2004	18	17	51%	9.2	62.5%
2005	16	15	52%	9.6	64.1%
2006	15	19	44%	9.5	63.1%
2007	13	20	39%	8.8	63.3%
2008	23	11	68%	9.9	62.4%
2009	11	16	41%	8.3	63.0%
TOTAL	96	98	49%	9.2	63.1%

Year	H Win	H Lose	Win%	Home R/G	Road R/G
2004	22	13	63%	4.8	4.4
2005	17	15	53%	4.8	4.8
2006	21	15	58%	5.0	4.4
2007	17	17	50%	4.3	4.5
2008	25	9	74%	5.7	4.3
2009	16	12	57%	4.4	4.1
TOTAL	118	81	59%	4.8	4.4

BOB DAVIDSON

Full name Robert Allan Davidson
Born August 3, 1952, Chicago, Illinois
Umpired First Game: May 31, 1982
Height: 6' 0" Weight: 230
Ejections: 1982 (1), 1983 (2), 1984 (7), 1985 (5), 1986 (3), 1987 (4), 1988 (7),
1989 (4), 1990 (16), 1991 (5), 1992 (3), 1993 (15), 1994 (5), 1995 (5), 1996 (9),
1997 (6), 1998 (5), 1999 (4), 2005 (2), 2006 (1), 2007 (6), 2008 (6), 2009 (7).
Total: 128

Davidson was nicknamed the "Patriotic Ump" by the foreign media thanks to his one-sided calls that favored the US in the 2006 World Baseball Classic. He has also been tagged with the "Balkin' Bob" label because of his fetish for calling balks. His strike zone tends to be wide but he doesn't often give pitchers the low strike.

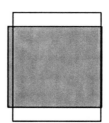

Year	Over	Under	%	Runs/Gm	Strike
2005	16	18	47%	9.3	63.7%
2006	18	18	50%	9.4	63.5%
2007	19	15	56%	9.2	63.0%
2008	11	22	33%	8.2	62.3%
2009	17	14	55%	9.9	63.8%
TOTAL	81	87	48%	9.2	63.3%

Year	H Win	H Lose	Win%	Home R/G	Road R/G
2005	16	19	46%	4.4	4.9
2006	17	20	46%	4.6	4.8
2007	20	14	59%	4.7	4.6
2008	19	16	54%	3.9	4.3
2009	16	17	48%	5.1	4.9
TOTAL	**88**	**86**	**51%**	**4.6**	**4.7**

GERRY DAVIS

Full name Gerald Sidney Davis
Born February 22, 1953, St. Louis, Missouri
Umpired First Game: June 9, 1982
Height: 6' 2" Weight: 225
Ejections: 1982 (1), 1986 (1), 1987 (1), 1988 (2), 1989 (7), 1990 (6), 1991 (3),
1992 (2), 1993 (3), 1994 (5), 1995 (3), 1996 (1), 1997 (2), 1999 (9), 2000 (5), 2001
(2), 2003 (7), 2004 (1), 2006 (1), 2007 (2), 2008 (1), 2009 (1). Total: 66

Davis is a long time major league umpire who has been calling MLB games in 1985. He has one of the smallest strike zones in the majors, and won't back down when players argue calls. Davis is not a very good umpire, and frequently makes mistakes while calling the bases. Davis owns www.gerrydavis.com, a sports store that concentrates primarily on umpire/referee equipment. His name has also been attached to a particular type of stance used by some umpires behind the plate. This stance has the umpire bending down only about three-quarters of the 'normal' way, with his/her back leaning slightly forward, and arms extended down, literally holding onto the top of the umpires leg guards. This has the advantage of getting the umpire's head slightly closer to the plate, plus saving wear and tear on the knees, while also giving support to the back.

Year	Over	Under	%	Runs/Gm	Strike
2004	14	16	47%	9.4	61.1%
2005	18	12	60%	9.6	62.3%
2006	16	16	50%	9.7	61.8%
2007	22	12	65%	11.7	61.7%
2008	17	15	53%	9.8	61.6%
2009	13	19	41%	9.5	61.6%
TOTAL	100	90	53%	10	61.7%

Year	H Win	H Lose	Win%	Home R/G	Road R/G
2004	13	18	42%	4.1	5.3
2005	18	14	56%	5.0	4.6
2006	15	19	44%	4.2	5.5
2007	17	18	49%	5.4	6.3
2008	20	13	61%	5.5	4.2
2009	18	16	53%	4.6	5.1
TOTAL	101	98	51%	4.8	5.2

DANA DEMUTH

Full name Dana Andrew DeMuth
Born May 30, 1956, Fremont, Ohio
Umpired First Game: June 3, 1983
Height: 6' 0" Weight: 230
Ejections: 1985 (2), 1987 (1), 1989 (1), 1990 (3), 1991 (2), 1992 (1), 1993 (2), 1994 (2), 1996 (1), 1997 (1), 1998 (2), 2000 (3), 2001 (2), 2002 (1), 2003 (1), 2004 (3), 2005 (2), 2006 (1), 2007 (2), 2008 (1), 2009 (0).
Total: 34

Demuth was born in Fremont Ohio and has been a major league umpire for 19 years. He is a very good umpire, and has earned respect around the league for both his calls on the field as well as his attitude towards players and managers. Demuth has worked in 11 post seasons, including the World Series in 1993, 1998, and 2001; the League Championship Series in 1991, 1995, 2000 and 2002; and the Division Series in 1996, 1997, 1999, and 2001. He also umpired in the All-Star Game in 1990 and 2001, working behind the plate for the second contest. Demuth has a small strike zone, and seems to have an aversion to calling low strikes.

Year	Over	Under	%	Runs/Gm	Strike
2004	19	12	61%	10.1	62.8%
2005	13	20	39%	8.4	63.6%
2006	13	9	59%	9.5	63.0%
2007	16	15	52%	10.5	61.7%
2008	13	19	41%	8.6	63.2%
2009	17	17	50%	9.9	61.5%
TOTAL	91	92	50%	9.5	62.6%

Year	H Win	H Lose	Win%	Home R/G	Road R/G
2004	22	12	65%	5.7	4.4
2005	15	19	44%	3.9	4.5
2006	10	13	43%	4.3	5.2
2007	17	17	50%	5.2	5.2
2008	12	21	36%	3.8	4.9
2009	18	16	53%	5.0	4.8
TOTAL	94	98	49%	4.6	4.9

LAZ DIAZ

Full name Lazaro Antonio Diaz
Born March 29, 1963, Miami, Florida
Umpired First Game: June 23, 1995
Height: 5' 11" Weight: 210
Ejections: 2000 (3), 2001 (4), 2002 (4), 2004 (1), 2005 (4), 2006 (1), 2007 (1),
2008 (2), 2009 (3).
Total: 23

Most fans know Diaz as the umpire that was attacked by a drunken Eric Dybas in 2003 while umpiring a game in Chicago. One of two Cuban-American umpires in the major leagues today (Angel Hernandez is the other), Diaz grew up in Miami and played high school ball with Danny Tartabull. After a stint in the Marines, Diaz played a few seasons of minor league ball for the Minnesota Twins, never making it above A ball before calling it quits. He became a full time major league umpire in 1999. He is a good umpire behind the plate, although he can be inconsistent at times in games.

Year	Over	Under	%	Runs/Gm	Strike
2004	15	19	44%	10	63.1%
2005	18	15	55%	10	62.5%
2006	12	22	35%	8.4	63.1%
2007	14	22	39%	8.3	64.4%
2008	17	14	55%	9.5	63.8%
2009	19	14	58%	10	63.0%
TOTAL	95	106	47%	9.4	63.3%

Year	H Win	H Lose	Win%	Home R/G	Road R/G
2004	22	13	63%	5.2	4.8
2005	17	16	52%	5.4	4.6
2006	24	11	69%	4.8	3.7
2007	19	17	53%	4.4	3.8
2008	21	13	62%	5.3	4.2
2009	14	19	42%	5.5	4.6
TOTAL	117	89	57%	5.1	4.3

MIKE DIMURO

Full name Michael Ryan DiMuro
Born October 12, 1967, Dunkirk, New York
Umpired First Game: July 31, 1997
Height: 6' 1" Weight: 190
Brother of Ray DiMuro
Son of Lou DiMuro
Ejections: 1999 (2), 2000 (8), 2001 (9), 2002 (3), 2003 (8), 2004 (7), 2005 (3),
2007 (3), 2008 (3). Total: 46

DiMuro comes from an umpiring background; his father Lou was an American League umpire from 1963 to 1982. He became a full-time umpire in 1999 and has quickly earned a reputation as one of the better umpires in the game. Before joining the majors, DiMuro signed a one-year contract with Japan to umpire its league games. The Japanese League, notorious for its atrocious umpiring, had hoped to DiMuro's hiring would help raise the standards and dignity of Japanese umpiring. This was a failure: DiMuro lasted only three months in Japan before the lack of support from the Japanese League management forced him to quit.

Year	Over	Under	%	Runs/Gm	Strike
2004	16	19	46%	9.5	62.8%
2005	20	9	69%	10.2	62.2%
2006	0	1	0%	9	65.4%
2007	2	6	25%	8.3	63.3%
2008	19	14	58%	9.3	62.5%
2009	15	18	45%	8.9	62.6%
TOTAL	72	67	52%	9.2	63.1%

Year	H Win	H Lose	Win%	Home R/G	Road R/G
2004	20	16	56%	4.6	4.9
2005	18	15	55%	5.7	4.5
2006	0	1	0%	3.0	6.0
2007	4	5	44%	3.4	4.9
2008	26	7	79%	5.7	3.6
2009	16	18	47%	4.5	4.4
TOTAL	84	62	58%	4.5	4.7

ROB DRAKE

Full name Robert Paul Drake
Born May 24, 1969, Indiana, Pennsylvania
Umpired First Game: September 3, 1999
Height: 5' 11" Weight: 210
Ejections: 2000 (3), 2001 (13), 2002 (2), 2003 (3), 2004 (7), 2005 (5), 2006 (2),
2007 (1), 2008 (4), 2009 (1).
Total: 41

Drake has a fairly large strike zone but doesn't give pitchers the low strike too often. Players usually know what they get from him; he seems to be pretty consistent from game to game regarding his strike zone.

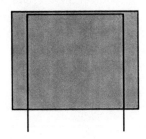

Year	Over	Under	%	Runs/Gm	Strike
2004	17	14	55%	9.8	62.4%
2005	15	14	52%	9.3	63.5%
2006	17	14	55%	10.3	62.8%
2007	16	18	47%	8.9	62.3%
2008	16	20	44%	8.7	63.2%
2009	19	19	50%	8.9	63.4%
TOTAL	100	99	50%	9.3	62.9%

Year	H Win	H Lose	Win%	Home R/G	Road R/G
2004	22	14	61%	5.3	4.5
2005	15	15	50%	4.7	4.6
2006	17	15	53%	5.8	4.6
2007	24	11	69%	5.0	3.9
2008	18	19	49%	4.2	4.4
2009	21	17	55%	4.5	4.4
TOTAL	117	91	56%	4.9	4.4

BRUCE DRECKMAN

Full name Bruce Michael Dreckman
Born August 7, 1970, Le Mars, Iowa Umpired First Game: April 5, 1996 Height:
6' 0" Weight: 240 Ejections: 1997 (1), 1999 (5), 2003 (2), 2004 (6), 2006 (4), 2007
(1), 2008 (1). Total: 20

Dreckman was one of the youngest major league umpires in history when he was
called up from AAA in 1997. After graduating high school, Dreckman went to
umpiring school and finished in the top 10% of the class, earning a spot in the
minor leagues. By the time he turned 26, he was in the major leagues to stay.
Except, of course, for the monumental stupid mistake Dreckman made when he
joined many fellow union members in submitting their resignation notice as a
bargaining tool. By the time Dreckman rescinded his resignation, he had already
been replaced. It took 2 years and an arbitration ruling in Dreckman's favor to
get him back behind the plate. He's a decent umpire, though thin-skinned at
times. His strike zone stretches a bit wider than usual, and doesn't seem fond of
low strikes.

Year	Over	Under	%	Runs/Gm	Strike
2004	16	14	53%	9.9	62.9%
2005	13	18	42%	9.2	63.5%
2006	19	13	59%	10.4	62.6%
2007	17	13	57%	9.8	62.8%
2008	14	19	42%	8.3	62.5%
2009	14	11	56%	9.8	62.9%
TOTAL	93	88	51%	9.6	62.9%

Year	H Win	H Lose	Win%	Home R/G	Road R/G
2004	18	15	55%	4.9	5.0
2005	19	14	58%	4.9	4.3
2006	19	15	56%	5.6	4.8
2007	13	17	43%	4.6	5.3
2008	19	14	58%	4.6	3.8
2009	13	13	50%	5.4	4.6
TOTAL	101	88	53%	4.9	4.8

DOUG EDDINGS

Full name Douglas Leon Eddings
Born September 14, 1968, Las Cruces, New Mexico
Umpired First Game: August 16, 1998
Height: 6' 0" Weight: 200
Ejections: 1999 (2), 2000 (10), 2001 (3), 2002 (7), 2003 (10), 2004 (5), 2005 (5),
2006 (4), 2007 (4), 2008 (4), 2009 (5). Total: 59

Like Don Denkinger, Doug Eddings' career will be remembered for blowing a call in one of baseball premier events. It is unfortunate, because he isn't a bad umpire. Eddings locked up, let the White Sox influence the call, and gave a poor performance in trying to explain away his decision in the post-game press conference. He has umpired in the major leagues since the 1999 season. Eddings has one of the largest strike zones in baseball, and his games naturally tend to go Under the total.

Year	Over	Under	%	Runs/Gm	Strike
2004	10	24	29%	7.3	64.7%
2005	11	20	35%	8.4	66.0%
2006	14	20	41%	7.9	65.1%
2007	15	19	44%	8.8	65.4%
2008	15	18	45%	9.6	63.8%
2009	17	17	50%	9.2	63.0%
TOTAL	82	118	41%	8.5	64.7%

Year	H Win	H Lose	Win%	Home R/G	Road R/G
2004	23	11	68%	4.3	3.0
2005	22	12	65%	4.7	3.7
2006	18	17	51%	3.9	4.1
2007	17	17	50%	4.3	4.4
2008	16	18	47%	4.5	5.1
2009	14	21	40%	4.3	4.9
TOTAL	110	96	53%	4.4	4.1

PAUL EMMEL

Full name Paul Lewis Emmel
Born May 2, 1968, Midland, Michigan
Umpired First Game: July 31, 1999
Height: 6' 2" Weight: 225
Ejections: 2000 (3), 2001 (3), 2002 (5), 2003 (3), 2004 (3), 2005 (1), 2006 (3),
2007 (6), 2008 (6). Total: 33

Emmel ended a game in 2004 by making one of the strangest calls I've seen in the Major Leagues. In the 10th inning of a game between Seattle and Tampa, Seattle shortstop Jose Lopez screened the runner on third trying to tag up after a short fly ball to left. The runner, Carl Crawford, made no attempt to go home, but Emmel still called obstruction and awarded Crawford home, giving the Devil Rays (and their bettors) the victory. Emmel obviously isn't afraid to make a call, but he also isn't afraid to bait players and stir up trouble. His strike zone tends to be slightly larger than usual, especially on low pitches.

Year	Over	Under	%	Runs/Gm	Strike
2004	15	19	44%	8.9	62.2%
2005	12	18	40%	8.1	63.6%
2006	18	12	60%	9.7	62.8%
2007	17	12	59%	9.4	63.1%
2008	13	20	39%	7.8	63.9%
2009	14	17	45%	9.3	62.6%
TOTAL	89	98	48%	8.9	63.0%

Year	H Win	H Lose	Win%	Home R/G	Road R/G
2004	19	15	56%	4.5	4.4
2005	21	13	62%	4.5	3.7
2006	21	10	68%	5.5	4.2
2007	18	11	62%	5.1	4.3
2008	18	15	55%	4.1	3.8
2009	16	17	48%	4.2	5.1
TOTAL	113	81	58%	4.8	4.1

MIKE ESTABROOK

Full name Michael Joseph Estabrook
Born July 28, 1976, Daytona Beach, Florida
Umpired First Game: May 7, 2006
Height: 6' 0" Weight: 195

Estabrook is a vacation umpire whose full time job has him contracted with the International League. So far he has been a very good pitcher's umpire. Beware of the small sample size, however.

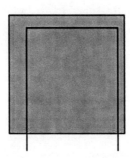

Year	Over	Under	%	Runs/Gm	Strike
2007	0	4	0%	5.2	66.5%
2008	7	15	32%	8.2	62.8%
2009	9	13	41%	8.6	62.4%
TOTAL	16	32	33%	8.5	63.5%

Year	H Win	H Lose	Win%	Home R/G	Road R/G
2007	3	1	75%	3.3	2.0
2008	12	10	55%	4.1	4.2
2009	8	15	35%	3.9	4.7
TOTAL	23	26	47%	4.3	4.1

MIKE EVERITT

Full name Mike G. Everitt
Born August 22, 1964, Gallup, New Mexico
Umpired First Game: June 20, 1996
Height: 6' 1" Weight: 194
Ejections: 1996 (1), 1997 (6), 1998 (2), 1999 (3), 2000 (13), 2001 (5), 2002 (4),
2004 (2), 2005 (6), 2006 (4), 2007 (7), 2008 (2), 2009 (3). Total: 58

Everitt is one of the best umpires in the game. He maintains control of games, and his games are always smooth running from start to finish. Everitt has only been umpiring in the majors since 1999, but has already worked a couple of playoff series and will likely be a playoff fixture in the future. He usually has a wide strike zone when calling games behind the plate, although his games did lean over in 2009.

Year	Over	Under	%	Runs/Gm	Strike
2004	13	17	43%	9.4	62.6%
2005	14	19	42%	8.4	64.3%
2006	21	13	62%	11.1	62.1%
2007	12	20	38%	8.4	62.9%
2008	15	16	48%	9.6	63.1%
2009	19	15	56%	9.8	62.1%
TOTAL	110	132	45%	8.7	63.2%

Year	H Win	H Lose	Win%	Home R/G	Road R/G
2004	17	13	57%	5.1	4.3
2005	17	17	50%	4.1	4.3
2006	13	21	38%	4.9	6.2
2007	22	12	65%	4.5	3.9
2008	23	13	64%	5.3	4.3
2009	23	11	68%	4.0	5.9
TOTAL	138	113	55%	4.4	4.3

CHAD FAIRCHILD

Full name Chadwick Jarrett Fairchild
Born December 30, 1970, Sandusky, Ohio
Umpired First Game: September 30, 2004
Height: 6' 3" Weight: 200
Ejections: 2005 (2), 2007 (7), 2008 (3), 2009 (3). Total: 15

Fairchild seems to have a large strike zone, but that isn't backed up by his Over/Under numbers. He has been umpiring at the professional ranks since 1997 and might be next in line when a full-time major league position opens up.

Year	Over	Under	%	Runs/Gm	Strike
2004	1	0	100%	10	61.0%
2005	5	7	42%	8.7	64.2%
2006	8	7	53%	8.7	62.7%
2007	14	13	52%	10.3	62.3%
2008	21	13	62%	11.1	61.8%
2009	13	21	38%	8.6	63.0%
TOTAL	**62**	**61**	**50%**	**9.6**	**62.5%**

Year	H Win	H Lose	Win%	Home R/G	Road R/G
2004	1	0	100%	6.0	4.0
2005	6	6	50%	4.9	3.8
2006	6	9	40%	4.2	4.5
2007	14	13	52%	5.2	5.0
2008	21	14	60%	5.8	5.3
2009	20	14	59%	4.4	4.2
TOTAL	**68**	**56**	**55%**	**5.1**	**4.5**

ANDY FLETCHER

Full name Andrew Jay Fletcher
Born November 17, 1966, Memphis, Tennessee
Umpired First Game: August 24, 1999
Height: 6' 1" Weight: 205
Ejections: 2001 (4), 2002 (3), 2003 (4), 2004 (6), 2005 (4), 2006 (1), 2007 (2),
2008 (8), 2009 (4). Total: 36

It is always a good show when Andy Fletcher decides to give a manager or player the boot. Fletcher has one of the best ejections style in the game today, with a leg kick that adds an explanation mark to the ejection. Fletcher has been umpiring in the major leagues since 1999. Overall, he is a very solid umpire. Pitchers love him.

Year	Over	Under	%	Runs/Gm	Strike
2004	17	12	59%	10	63.5%
2005	14	18	44%	9.6	63.1%
2006	17	15	53%	10.8	61.3%
2007	4	13	24%	7.2	63.7%
2008	11	17	39%	8.1	61.9%
2009	10	21	32%	8.3	62.2%
TOTAL	73	96	43%	9	62.6%

Year	H Win	H Lose	Win%	Home R/G	Road R/G
2004	18	14	56%	5.2	4.8
2005	22	12	65%	5.0	4.7
2006	16	16	50%	5.0	5.8
2007	9	9	50%	3.3	3.9
2008	16	16	50%	3.8	4.3
2009	19	15	56%	4.3	4.1
TOTAL	100	82	55%	4.4	4.6

MARTY FOSTER

Full name Martin Robert Foster
Born November 25, 1963, Denver, Colorado
Umpired First Game: September 10, 1996
Height: 5' 11" Weight: 210
Ejections: 1998 (5), 1999 (7), 2000 (4), 2001 (5), 2002 (3), 2003 (5), 2004 (9),
2005 (14), 2006 (2), 2007 (3), 2008 (6), 2009 (4). Total: 67

Foster had some troubles with the Yankees in 2009. Derek Jeter claimed Foster called him out during an attempted steal, saying "if the ball beats you, you're out." He tossed A-Rod out of the game later in the season after Rodriguez kept arguing a called third strike. Foster's games tend to go under when he is behind home plate.

Year	Over	Under	%	Runs/Gm	Strike
2004	12	21	36%	9.5	62.5%
2005	11	19	37%	8.3	62.7%
2006	18	12	60%	11.1	63.5%
2007	13	17	43%	9.9	62.9%
2008	11	22	33%	8.4	63.5%
2009	11	17	39%	8.8	62.5%
TOTAL	76	108	41%	9.3	62.9%

Year	H Win	H Lose	Win%	Home R/G	Road R/G
2004	17	16	52%	4.8	4.7
2005	15	17	47%	4.4	3.9
2006	16	17	48%	5.6	5.6
2007	11	20	35%	4.0	5.9
2008	16	19	46%	3.7	4.7
2009	18	13	58%	4.8	4.0
TOTAL	93	102	48%	4.4	4.9

GREG GIBSON

Full name Gregory Allen Gibson
Born October 2, 1968, Ironton, Ohio
Umpired First Game: June 14, 1997
Height: 5' 10" Weight: 190
Ejections: 1997 (1), 1998 (2), 1999 (7), 2000 (5), 2001 (5), 2002 (5), 2003 (4),
2004 (1), 2005 (3), 2006 (4), 2007 (4), 2008 (2), 2009 (5).
Total: 48

Gibson has umpired full-time in the majors since 1999. After graduating from Shawnee State University, he landed a job in the Appalachian League and worked his way up from there. Overall, he is a pretty good umpire. He does, however, have a quick fuse and tends to take offense at perceived slights from players and managers. Gibson's strike zone varies from game to game, but usually is consistent once the game begins.

Year	Over	Under	%	Runs/Gm	Strike
2005	15	15	50%	9.8	62.0%
2006	18	17	51%	10.3	61.1%
2007	16	14	53%	10.5	61.0%
2008	16	16	50%	9.5	61.8%
2009	15	11	58%	10	62.4%
TOTAL	98	86	53%	10.1	61.6%

Year	H Win	H Lose	Win%	Home R/G	Road R/G
2004	14	19	42%	4.6	5.9
2005	21	12	64%	5.4	4.5
2006	21	15	58%	5.4	4.8
2007	19	15	56%	5.2	5.4
2008	18	18	50%	4.6	4.9
2009	14	14	50%	5.6	4.5
TOTAL	107	93	54%	5.3	5.0

BRIAN GORMAN

Full name Brian Scott Gorman
Born June 11, 1959, Whitestone, New York
Umpired First Game: April 24, 1991
Height: 6' 1" Weight: 200
Son of Tom Gorman
Ejections: 1992 (1), 1993 (3), 1994 (3), 1995 (4), 1996 (2), 1997 (3), 1998 (2),
1999 (3), 2000 (1), 2001 (2), 2002 (3), 2003 (5), 2004 (3), 2005 (1), 2006 (1), 2008
(1), 2009 (2).
Total: 40

Gorman has been umpiring in the major leagues since 1993. He has both umpiring and baseball blood running through his veins; his dad, Tom, played for the New York Giants and was a National League umpire from 1951 to 1976. Gorman has one of the biggest strike zones in baseball, but is a solid umpire in all phases of the game. He consistently umpires in post-season games, an indication that MLB believes in Gorman's competence as well.

Year	Over	Under	%	Runs/Gm	Strike
2004	9	24	27%	7.6	62.1%
2005	12	18	40%	8.3	63.3%
2006	14	17	45%	8.7	63.7%
2007	19	14	58%	10.8	63.2%
2008	16	15	52%	9.4	63.9%
2009	13	19	41%	8.4	63.2%
TOTAL	83	107	44%	8.9	63.2%

Year	H Win	H Lose	Win%	Home R/G	Road R/G
2004	17	19	47%	3.6	4.0
2005	22	10	69%	4.8	3.6
2006	15	18	45%	4.1	4.7
2007	18	16	53%	5.2	5.7
2008	25	9	74%	5.0	4.4
2009	15	18	45%	3.7	4.6
TOTAL	112	90	55%	4.6	4.4

CHRIS GUCCIONE

Full name Christopher Gene Guccione
Born June 24, 1974, Salida, Colorado
Umpired First Game: April 25, 2000
Height: 5' 9" Weight: 220
Ejections: 2000 (3), 2001 (2), 2002 (6), 2003 (4), 2004 (7), 2005 (8), 2006 (4),
2007 (6), 2008 (3), 2009 (4).
Total: 47

Guccione was finally named a full-time major league umpire in 2009 after fourteen years in the minors, including eight as an vacation umpire for the major leagues. His games tended to go under in 2009, but his history shows that he doesn't have a lasting trend behind the plate.

Year	Over	Under	%	Runs/Gm	Strike
2004	16	14	53%	10.2	62.9%
2005	12	17	41%	8.7	63.6%
2006	21	10	68%	10.8	62.5%
2007	19	20	49%	8.9	62.1%
2008	17	16	52%	9.8	62.7%
2009	12	20	38%	8.1	62.6%
TOTAL	**97**	**97**	**50%**	**9.4**	**62.7%**

Year	H Win	H Lose	Win%	Home R/G	Road R/G
2004	21	10	68%	5.7	4.4
2005	13	16	45%	4.4	4.3
2006	20	13	61%	5.6	5.3
2007	23	17	58%	4.8	4.2
2008	21	16	57%	4.9	5.0
2009	16	17	48%	4.2	4.1
TOTAL	**114**	**89**	**56%**	**4.9**	**4.6**

TOM HALLION

Full name Thomas Francis Hallion
Born September 5, 1956, Saugerties, New York
Umpired First Game: June 10, 1985
Height: 5' 10" Weight: 185
Ejections: 1986 (5), 1987 (6), 1988 (2), 1989 (11), 1990 (1), 1991 (3), 1992 (4),
1994 (5), 1995 (2), 1996 (3), 1997 (6), 1998 (2), 1999 (2), 2005 (2), 2006 (2), 2007
(7), 2008 (1), 2009 (2). Total: 66

Hallion has a pretty good sized strike zone, but it does lack consistency at times.
He usually tends towards the Under when behind home plate.

Year	Over	Under	%	Runs/Gm	Strike
2005	11	18	38%	9.3	62.7%
2006	14	18	44%	8.5	62.7%
2007	18	15	55%	9.8	63.0%
2008	14	19	42%	9	62.5%
2009	16	15	52%	8.9	62.0%
TOTAL	73	85	46%	9.1	62.6%

Year	H Win	H Lose	Win%	Home R/G	Road R/G
2005	19	14	58%	4.8	4.5
2006	25	9	74%	4.9	3.6
2007	15	18	45%	4.7	5.1
2008	17	17	50%	4.5	4.5
2009	17	16	52%	4.6	4.2
TOTAL	93	74	56%	4.7	4.4

ANGEL HERNANDEZ

Full name Angel Hernandez
Born August 26, 1961, Havana, Cuba
Umpired First Game: May 23, 1991
Height: 6' 2" Weight: 198
Ejections: 1992 (1), 1993 (1), 1994 (5), 1995 (3), 1996 (4), 1997 (1), 1998 (2),
1999 (2), 2001 (3), 2002 (5), 2003 (4), 2004 (3), 2005 (4), 2006 (7), 2007 (4), 2008
(4), 2009 (4). Total: 57

Hernandez is not a very good umpire. At times his strike zone wobbles from inning to inning. When he is on, he is great behind the plate. When he's off, look out. Hernandez is a bit of a hothead, which inflames players and managers alike once he starts blowing calls. He has been a major league umpire since 1993. Born in Havana in 1961, Hernandez is the first Cuban-born umpire in the major leagues. Overall, Hernandez has been an under umpire, but his strike zone is too inconsistent for me to get much more of a read on it.

Year	Over	Under	%	Runs/Gm	Strike
2004	14	15	48%	10	62.8%
2005	11	17	39%	9.2	63.4%
2006	16	18	47%	9.1	62.6%
2007	18	15	55%	10.1	62.0%
2008	11	21	34%	8.5	62.4%
2009	18	16	53%	9.3	62.3%
TOTAL	88	102	46%	9.4	62.6%

Year	H Win	H Lose	Win%	Home R/G	Road R/G
2004	19	13	59%	5.1	4.8
2005	12	17	41%	3.9	5.3
2006	18	16	53%	4.2	4.8
2007	26	10	72%	5.7	4.3
2008	26	9	74%	5.3	3.3
2009	21	14	60%	4.5	4.8
TOTAL	122	79	61%	4.8	4.6

ED HICKOX

Full name Edwin William Hickox
Born July 31, 1962, Deland, Florida
Umpired First Game: May 16, 1990
Height: 5' 11" Weight: 185
Ejections: 1990 (9), 1994 (3), 1996 (2), 1997 (3), 1998 (5), 1999 (2), 2005 (1), 2007 (2). Total: 27

Hickox was hit by a foul ball early in the 2009 season, suffering his second serious concussion of his career. He sat out the rest of the MLB season, but is expected to be back in 2010.

Year	Over	Under	%	Runs/Gm	Strike
2005	14	11	56%	9.3	62.8%
2006	19	11	63%	10.3	62.4%
2007	12	19	39%	8.9	62.4%
2008	15	15	50%	9.5	62.2%
2009	1	2	33%	14.3	58.9%
TOTAL	61	58	51%	10.5	61.7%

Year	H Win	H Lose	Win%	Home R/G	Road R/G
2005	15	11	58%	5.2	4.2
2006	16	16	50%	4.7	5.7
2007	16	18	47%	4.2	4.8
2008	14	17	45%	4.6	4.9
2009	2	1	67%	8.3	6.0
TOTAL	63	63	50%	5.4	5.1

BILL HOHN

Full name William John Hohn
Born June 29, 1955, Butler, Pennsylvania
Umpired First Game: May 29, 1987
Height: 6' 0" Weight: 180
Ejections: 1989 (5), 1990 (4), 1991 (2), 1992 (2), 1993 (10), 1994 (2), 1995 (7),
1996 (4), 1997 (2), 1998 (4), 1999 (5), 2002 (2), 2003 (5), 2004 (6), 2005 (5), 2008
(8), 2009 (9). Total: 82

Hohn has a relatively large strike zone, and has seen his games go Under a majority of the time in recent years. He is kind of a hot head and has his fair share of ejections.

Year	Over	Under	%	Runs/Gm	Strike
2004	21	11	66%	10.4	62.0%
2005	13	20	39%	8.7	62.3%
2007	2	1	67%	9.7	59.0%
2008	9	16	36%	7.5	62.5%
2009	11	12	48%	8.7	61.8%
TOTAL	**56**	**60**	**48%**	**9.0**	**61.5%**

Year	H Win	H Lose	Win%	Home R/G	Road R/G
2004	14	19	42%	4.7	5.7
2005	13	20	39%	3.8	4.9
2007	2	1	67%	5.3	4.3
2008	9	17	35%	3.3	4.2
2009	12	12	50%	4.8	3.8
TOTAL	**50**	**69**	**42%**	**4.4**	**4.6**

SAM HOLBROOK

Full name Samuel Woodford Holbrook
Born July 7, 1965, Morehead, Kentucky
Umpired First Game: June 26, 1996
Height: 6' 1" Weight: 230
Ejections: 1998 (8), 1999 (1), 2003 (1), 2004 (3), 2005 (3), 2006 (11), 2007 (5),
2008 (3), 2009 (1).
Total: 36

Holbrooke has umpired in the major leagues since 1998; he first began umpiring professionally in 1990. A baseball player in college for four years, Holbrooke received a Master's degree from Eastern Kentucky University before making umpiring his career. He isn't a good umpire overall, but does a respectable job behind the plate. He was another umpire that regained his job with an arbitrator ruled MLB couldn't fire him during the labor trouble of 1999. A solid under umpire his first few years up, Holbrooke has went over in the majority of his games since. He will call the high strike, but doesn't help out pitchers who work low in the zone.

Year	Over	Under	%	Runs/Gm	Strike
2004	15	16	48%	10.2	62.3%
2005	19	11	63%	10.6	63.2%
2006	19	11	63%	10.3	61.7%
2007	19	13	59%	10.8	62.1%
2008	20	14	59%	10.6	62.2%
2009	14	19	42%	8.4	62.6%
TOTAL	**106**	**84**	**56%**	**10.2**	**62.4%**

Year	H Win	H Lose	Win%	Home R/G	Road R/G
2004	19	13	59%	5.2	5.0
2005	20	15	57%	5.5	5.1
2006	13	17	43%	5.0	5.4
2007	20	14	59%	5.4	5.4
2008	21	13	62%	5.8	4.8
2009	19	15	56%	4.6	4.0
TOTAL	**112**	**87**	**56%**	**5.2**	**5.1**

JAMES HOYE

Full name James Patrick Hoye
Born February 8, 1971, Parma, Ohio
Umpired First Game: June 8, 2003
Height: 6' 0" Weight: 185
Ejections: 2004 (3), 2006 (1), 2007 (3), 2008 (3).
Total: 10

Hoye's games have tended to go under when he's behind the plate, but his strike zone isn't anything out of the ordinary.

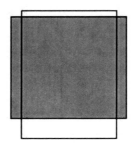

Year	Over	Under	%	Runs/Gm	Strike
2004	5	9	36%	8.8	61.2%
2005	8	6	57%	11.3	62.5%
2006	12	8	60%	9.8	62.9%
2007	19	13	59%	10.7	62.3%
2008	17	18	49%	10.0	61.6%
2009	14	25	36%	8.8	62.0%
TOTAL	**75**	**79**	**49%**	**9.9**	**62.1%**

Year	H Win	H Lose	Win%	Home R/G	Road R/G
2004	3	11	21%	3.0	5.8
2005	5	11	31%	4.9	6.4
2006	11	9	55%	5.2	4.6
2007	15	20	43%	5.2	5.6
2008	22	16	58%	5.1	5.0
2009	21	20	51%	4.4	4.4
TOTAL	**77**	**87**	**47%**	**4.6**	**5.3**

MARVIN HUDSON

Full name Marvin Lee Hudson
Born March 3, 1964, Marietta, Georgia
Umpired First Game: July 29, 1998
Height: 5' 10" Weight: 215
Ejections: 2000 (1), 2001 (3), 2002 (4), 2003 (2), 2004 (5), 2005 (2), 2006 (2),
2007 (1), 2008 (2), 2009 (4).
Total: 26

Hudson was catcher at Piedmont College for four years before graduating in
1986. A full time major league umpire since 1999, Hudson's eyes are taken care
of by his wife, who owns an optical shop in Washington Georgia. Hudson has a
small strike zone, but is a decent umpire.

Year	Over	Under	%	Runs/Gm	Strike
2004	16	18	47%	9.9	62.5%
2005	19	15	56%	10	63.5%
2006	12	19	39%	8.6	62.6%
2007	15	15	50%	9.0	62.1%
2008	21	13	62%	10.1	61.7%
2009	19	14	58%	8.4	62.6%
TOTAL	102	94	52%	9.3	62.5%

Year	H Win	H Lose	Win%	Home R/G	Road R/G
2004	21	16	57%	5.1	4.8
2005	16	19	46%	4.9	5.1
2006	19	13	59%	4.8	3.8
2007	11	21	34%	4.0	5.0
2008	19	15	56%	5.2	4.9
2009	20	15	57%	4.7	3.7
TOTAL	106	99	52%	4.6	4.7

DAN IASSOGNA

Full name Daniel Ralph Iassogna
Born May 3, 1969, Bridgeport, Connecticut
Umpired First Game: August 20, 1999
Height: 5' 10" Weight: 190
Ejections: 1999 (1), 2000 (2), 2001 (4), 2002 (10), 2003 (4), 2004 (5), 2005 (7),
2006 (4), 2007 (4), 2008 (4). Total: 45

Iassogna made some news a few years ago when he tossed Greg Gagne from a game after ruling Gagne intentionally hit Adam Dunn with a pitch while the Dodgers were up two runs in the ninth inning. In 2008, Marlon Anderson accused Iassogna of lying after being ejected for arguing a called third strike. "I went in there today and read the report that he wrote," Anderson said. "It's amazing that a grown man could sit there and lie and say the things that he said and not have to show up and defend what he said." Iassogna has a very high strike zone.

Year	Over	Under	%	Runs/Gm	Strike
2004	16	14	53%	10.1	62.7%
2005	18	17	51%	9.1	62.4%
2006	13	19	41%	8.8	62.8%
2007	17	15	53%	9.8	62.7%
2008	17	17	50%	8.5	63.2%
2009	21	13	62%	10.6	62.6%
TOTAL	**102**	**95**	**52%**	**9.5**	**62.7%**

Year	H Win	H Lose	Win%	Home R/G	Road R/G
2004	18	14	56%	5.3	4.8
2005	22	13	63%	4.8	4.3
2006	15	19	44%	4.7	4.2
2007	23	11	68%	5.7	4.2
2008	19	15	56%	4.6	3.9
2009	17	17	50%	5.3	5.3
TOTAL	**114**	**89**	**56%**	**5.1**	**4.5**

ADRIAN JOHNSON

Full name Adrian Andre Johnson
Born May 25, 1975, Houston, Texas
Umpired First Game: April 19, 2006
Height: 5' 9" Weight: 210
Ejections: 2008 (4)

Johnson has been a vacation umpire since 2006. His strike zone is small and tends to be inconsistent, although inexperience might get a big chunk of the blame.

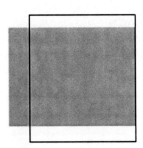

Year	Over	Under	%	Runs/Gm	Strike
2006	0	1	0%	5	61.2%
2007	7	8	47%	9	62.2%
2008	19	15	56%	9.8	61.8%
2009	16	14	53%	9.7	61.4%
TOTAL	**42**	**38**	**53%**	**8.4**	**61.7%**

Year	H Win	H Lose	Win%	Home R/G	Road R/G
2006	1	0	100%	5.0	-
2007	9	7	56%	4.4	4.6
2008	18	18	50%	4.5	5.3
2009	24	11	69%	3.8	5.9
TOTAL	**52**	**36**	**59%**	**4.4**	**5.3**

JIM JOYCE

Full name James A. III Joyce
Born October 3, 1955, Toledo, Ohio
Umpired First Game: May 23, 1987
Height: 6' 0" Weight: 190
Ejections: 1989 (3), 1990 (7), 1991 (2), 1992 (7), 1993 (4), 1994 (1), 1995 (3),
1996 (2), 1997 (6), 1998 (4), 1999 (1), 2000 (4), 2001 (4), 2002 (2), 2003 (2), 2004
(3), 2005 (1), 2007 (1), 2008 (2), 2009 (3). Total: 62

Joyce is one of the outstanding umpires in the game today. He has been in the major leagues since 1989 and consistently works playoff series in October. Born in 1955, Joyce played baseball and received a degree in Education at Bowling Green University. From Toledo Ohio, Joyce currently lives in Beaverton Oregon. He has an extremely consistent strike zone.

Year	Over	Under	%	Runs/Gm	Strike
2004	16	16	50%	9.5	62.8%
2005	5	10	33%	9.6	63.5%
2006	17	17	50%	10.5	62.8%
2007	18	16	53%	9.6	61.6%
2008	17	15	53%	9.6	63.5%
2009	13	18	42%	9.2	61.6%
TOTAL	86	92	48%	9.7	62.6%

Year	H Win	H Lose	Win%	Home R/G	Road R/G
2004	15	17	47%	4.7	4.8
2005	10	7	59%	5.0	4.7
2006	17	19	47%	5.1	5.4
2007	17	17	50%	4.4	5.2
2008	19	16	54%	4.8	4.8
2009	18	15	55%	4.6	4.6
TOTAL	96	91	51%	4.8	4.9

JEFF KELLOGG

Full name Jeffrey William Kellogg
Born August 29, 1961, Coldwater, Michigan
Umpired First Game: June 12, 1991
Height: 6' 0" Weight: 205
Ejections: 1992 (2), 1993 (3), 1994 (1), 1995 (3), 1996 (3), 1997 (2), 1998 (3),
1999 (3), 2003 (2), 2004 (1), 2006 (1), 2007 (1), 2008 (4). Total: 29

Kellogg has umpired in the major leagues since 1993. A graduate of Ferris State University with a degree in criminal science, Kellogg puts the degree to good use in maintaining control over a baseball game. He is an excellent umpire with a very good strike zone. The tendency towards under in 2009 is most likely a fluke, although it is something to watch next season.

Year	Over	Under	%	Runs/Gm	Strike
2004	19	13	59%	10.1	61.8%
2005	4	9	31%	7.1	62.7%
2006	17	15	53%	9.8	63.2%
2007	15	19	44%	9.3	62.0%
2008	18	16	53%	9.4	62.2%
2009	9	23	28%	7.6	61.5%
TOTAL	82	95	46%	8.9	62.2%

Year	H Win	H Lose	Win%	Home R/G	Road R/G
2004	19	15	56%	5.2	4.9
2005	8	5	62%	4.1	3.0
2006	18	14	56%	5.2	4.6
2007	21	14	60%	4.8	4.4
2008	22	12	65%	4.9	4.6
2009	17	17	50%	3.5	4.1
TOTAL	105	77	58%	4.6	4.3

BRIAN KNIGHT

Full name Brian Michael Knight
Born October 2, 1974, Helena, Montana
Umpired First Game: May 7, 2001
Height: 6' 0" Weight: 190
Ejections: 2004 (1), 2006 (2), 2007 (5), 2008 (1). Total: 9

A vacation umpire since 2004, Knight seems to have a small strike zone.

Year	Over	Under	%	Runs/Gm	Strike
2004	4	5	44%	8.7	63.6%
2005	4	4	50%	7.7	63.7%
2006	5	5	50%	8.1	62.1%
2007	14	13	52%	10	62.5%
2008	12	22	35%	8.8	62.0%
2009	18	16	53%	10	61.9%
TOTAL	**57**	**65**	**47%**	**8.9**	**62.6%**

Year	H Win	H Lose	Win%	Home R/G	Road R/G
2004	6	3	67%	4.2	4.4
2005	5	4	56%	4.0	3.7
2006	5	5	50%	3.6	4.5
2007	18	10	64%	5.8	4.2
2008	21	13	62%	4.9	3.9
2009	19	16	54%	5.2	4.9
TOTAL	**74**	**51**	**59%**	**4.6**	**4.3**

RON KULPA

Full name Ronald Clarence Kulpa
Born October 5, 1968, St. Louis, Missouri
Umpired First Game: July 23, 1998
Height: 6' 2" Weight: 220
Ejections: 1999 (2), 2000 (2), 2001 (6), 2002 (1), 2003 (3), 2004 (2), 2005 (3),
2006 (3), 2007 (3), 2008 (3), 2009 (3). Total: 31.

Kulpa is an avid hockey player, a skill that likely came in handy a few years back when Carl Everett head-butted Kulpa during an argument. Kulpa is not a very good umpire, and he compounds that by being confrontational to players that disagree with calls. His games tend to go under.

Year	Over	Under	%	Runs/Gm	Strike
2004	14	17	45%	9.9	62.1%
2005	13	18	42%	8.3	62.7%
2006	13	18	42%	8.8	62.6%
2007	16	16	50%	9.6	63.6%
2008	10	21	32%	7.8	63.1%
2009	9	13	41%	9.0	62.9%
TOTAL	**75**	**103**	**42%**	**8.9**	**62.8%**

Year	H Win	H Lose	Win%	Home R/G	Road R/G
2004	17	17	50%	5.2	4.8
2005	16	19	46%	4.0	4.3
2006	23	10	70%	5.3	3.5
2007	22	13	63%	5.3	4.3
2008	21	11	66%	4.2	3.6
2009	12	11	52%	4.8	4.3
TOTAL	**111**	**81**	**58%**	**4.8**	**4.1**

JERRY LAYNE

Full name Jerry Blake Layne
Born September 28, 1958, Pikeville, Kentucky
Umpired First Game: April 19, 1989
Height: 6' 4" Weight: 255
Ejections: 1989 (2), 1990 (7), 1991 (1), 1992 (1), 1993 (5), 1994 (4), 1995 (3), 1996 (11), 1997 (8), 1998 (2), 1999 (3), 2000 (2), 2002 (4), 2003 (3), 2004 (2), 2005 (1), 2006 (2), 2007 (5). Total: 66

An umpire since 1989, Layne was born in Pikeville Kentucky on September 28, 1958. He is not a very good umpire; his strike zone is small and inconsistent; Layne's refusal to call the high strike can be frustrating at times. He also has a nasty temper. When a player begins to squawk, Layne will go after that player and tends to inflame a bad situation.

Year	Over	Under	%	Runs/Gm	Strike
2004	7	12	37%	9.1	60.5%
2005	16	15	52%	9.7	61.6%
2006	16	18	47%	10.1	62.3%
2007	8	9	47%	9.9	61.1%
2008	15	16	48%	9.4	61.4%
2009	12	19	39%	8.0	62.7%
TOTAL	**74**	**89**	**45%**	**9.4**	**61.6%**

Year	H Win	H Lose	Win%	Home R/G	Road R/G
2004	12	8	60%	5.1	4.1
2005	16	18	47%	5.0	4.7
2006	22	13	63%	5.1	5.1
2007	12	7	63%	5.4	4.5
2008	16	16	50%	4.5	4.9
2009	20	13	61%	4.1	3.8
TOTAL	**98**	**75**	**57%**	**4.9**	**4.5**

ALFONSO MARQUEZ

Full name Alfonso Marquez
Born April 12, 1972, Zacatecas, Zacatecas (Mexico)
Umpired First Game: August 13, 1999
Height: 5' 11" Weight: 200
Ejections: 1999 (2), 2000 (2), 2001 (3), 2002 (4), 2003 (2), 2004 (5), 2005 (4),
2006 (3), 2007 (6), 2008 (4). Total: 35

Marquez made a rapid move through the minor league umpiring system. Born in Zacatecas Mexico, Marquez joined the major league staff in 1999 at the age of 25. He is the first Mexican-born umpire in the major leagues. In his free time, he started a foundation that distributes sports equipment to children in Mexico. He has umpired the 2006 World Series, the 2003 American League Championship Series, and four Division Series (2001, 2002, 2005, 2006), as well as the 2006 All-Star Game.

Year	Over	Under	%	Runs/Gm	Strike
2004	16	17	48%	9.7	61.1%
2005	11	20	35%	8.6	62.1%
2006	17	15	53%	9.6	62.7%
2007	14	15	48%	8.9	62.5%
2008	19	13	59%	10.2	61.9%
2009	1	1	50%	10	61.6%
TOTAL	78	81	49%	9.5	62.0%

Year	H Win	H Lose	Win%	Home R/G	Road R/G
2004	18	17	51%	5.5	4.3
2005	16	17	48%	4.1	4.5
2006	19	15	56%	5.1	4.5
2007	20	11	65%	4.8	4.1
2008	19	15	56%	5.6	4.6
2009	1	1	50%	5.0	5.0
TOTAL	93	76	55%	5.0	4.5

RANDY MARSH

Full name Randall Gilbert Marsh
Born April 8, 1949, Covington, Kentucky
Umpired First Game: May 22, 1981
Height: 6' 0" Weight: 220
Ejections: 1981 (1), 1982 (5), 1983 (1), 1984 (1), 1987 (3), 1988 (2), 1991 (4),
1992 (2), 1993 (1), 1994 (2), 1996 (4), 1997 (1), 1998 (2), 1999 (1), 2002 (5), 2003
(4), 2005 (4), 2006 (2). Total: 45

Marsh's resume should tell you all you need to know about his ability as an umpire. He is a very good umpire that shows respect for everyone in the game. His strike zone is small but extremely consistent; his games do lean Over. He has umpired in the World Series in 1990, 1997, 1999, 2003 and 2006, serving as crew chief for the last three Series, and in the All-Star Game in 1985, 1988, 1996 and 2006.. He is the tenth umpire in history to serve as crew chief for three World Series. He has also worked in seven League Championship Series and five Division Series.

Year	Over	Under	%	Runs/Gm	Strike
2004	15	9	63%	10	61.6%
2005	20	14	59%	10	62.4%
2006	15	16	48%	9.6	61.8%
2007	15	18	45%	9.1	61.6%
2008	9	10	47%	10.5	61.5%
2009	20	12	63%	10.2	61.9%
TOTAL	94	79	54%	9.9	61.8%

Year	H Win	H Lose	Win%	Home R/G	Road R/G
2004	15	10	60%	5.0	5.0
2005	18	17	51%	4.9	5.2
2006	22	12	65%	5.0	4.6
2007	18	16	53%	4.7	4.4
2008	9	10	47%	4.7	5.8
2009	18	14	56%	5.2	5.0
TOTAL	100	79	56%	5.0	4.9

TIM MCCLELLAND

Full name Timothy Reid McClelland
Born December 12, 1951, Jackson, Michigan
Umpired First Game: September 3, 1981
Height: 6' 6" Weight: 250
Ejections: 1982 (1), 1983 (5), 1984 (5), 1985 (4), 1986 (3), 1988 (2), 1989 (3),
1990 (4), 1991 (3), 1992 (1), 1993 (2), 1994 (2), 1995 (2), 1996 (1), 1997 (4), 1998
(1), 1999 (2), 2000 (5), 2001 (2), 2002 (3), 2003 (3), 2004 (2), 2005 (3), 2006 (1),
2007 (4), 2008 (3). Total: 71

McClelland was thought by many in the game to be the best umpire in baseball...that opinion may have changed after a few well-publicized mistakes in 2009. He joined the major league crew in 1983. You can often see a young McClelland calling George Brett out in the infamous Pine-Tar game that year. McClelland has a habit of being in the wrong place at the wrong time when it comes to illegal bats; he was also on the umpiring crews when Albert Belle and Sammy Sosa were busted with corked bats. McClelland has a very consistent strike zone, although his delay in making the strike calls can be a bit frustrating at times to a fan watching on TV.

Year	Over	Under	%	Runs/Gm	Strike
2004	16	13	55%	10	61.5%
2005	14	20	41%	9.4	61.0%
2006	19	15	56%	10.3	61.0%
2007	13	19	41%	9.4	62.9%
2008	20	14	59%	10.6	61.6%
2009	20	14	59%	11.1	60.5%
TOTAL	102	95	52%	10.1	61.4%

Year	H Win	H Lose	Win%	Home R/G	Road R/G
2004	16	13	55%	5.2	4.9
2005	19	15	56%	4.7	4.7
2006	18	16	53%	5.2	5.1
2007	23	14	62%	5.2	4.2
2008	22	13	63%	5.4	5.2
2009	17	19	47%	5.9	5.3
TOTAL	115	90	56%	5.3	4.9

JERRY MEALS

Full name Gerald William Meals
Born October 20, 1961, Butler, Pennsylvania
Umpired First Game: September 14, 1992
Height: 5' 8" Weight: 168
Ejections: 1995 (2), 1997 (1), 1998 (5), 1999 (2), 2000 (2), 2001 (4), 2002 (2),
2003 (4), 2006 (3), 2007 (3), 2008 (3).
Total: 31

Meals has been a major league umpire since 1998. Born in 1961, he currently lives in Salem Ohio with his wife and five children. He is a poor umpire. Meals lacks consistency both as a home plate umpire and on the bases. His strike zone is pretty varies at times and he doesn't give a pitcher the low strike. He was a pretty solid under umpire until the 2008 season.

Year	Over	Under	%	Runs/Gm	Strike
2004	14	21	40%	9.1	61.6%
2005	16	18	47%	10.2	62.9%
2006	14	16	47%	9.8	62.6%
2007	12	17	41%	9.8	62.3%
2008	22	12	65%	9.8	62.2%
2009	18	15	55%	9.8	62.9%
TOTAL	96	99	49%	9.8	62.4%

Year	H Win	H Lose	Win%	Home R/G	Road R/G
2004	21	15	58%	4.4	4.8
2005	18	17	51%	5.2	5.0
2006	24	10	71%	5.3	4.5
2007	15	17	47%	4.8	5.0
2008	15	19	44%	4.5	5.4
2009	16	18	47%	4.6	5.1
TOTAL	109	96	53%	4.8	5.0

CHUCK MERIWETHER

Full name Julius Edward Meriwether
Born June 30, 1956, Nashville, Tennessee
Umpired First Game: May 23, 1987
Height: 6' 5" Weight: 230
Ejections: 1991 (3), 1992 (1), 1993 (3), 1995 (2), 1997 (1), 1999 (5), 2000 (3),
2001 (1), 2003 (1), 2004 (2), 2007 (3), 2008 (1).
Total: 26

Meriwether is a lesson in perseverance. After graduating from Athens State College in 1978, he began working as an umpire in the Midwest League. 14 years later, including eleven at AAA, Meriwether finally earned a major league spot in 1993. He isn't a good umpire; watching him work games behind the plate can be confusing to pitchers, batters, and fans. He does, however, show respect for the game and doesn't go out of his way to instigate problems with players and managers.

Year	Over	Under	%	Runs/Gm	Strike
2004	21	15	58%	10.7	61.5%
2005	15	17	47%	9.2	62.6%
2006	10	20	33%	8.8	61.6%
2007	16	14	53%	9.6	62.2%
2008	12	21	36%	8.9	62.8%
2009	18	17	51%	10.0	63.0%
TOTAL	92	104	47%	9.5	62.3%

Year	H Win	H Lose	Win%	Home R/G	Road R/G
2004	23	14	62%	5.5	5.2
2005	21	13	62%	4.7	4.6
2006	14	19	42%	4.2	4.6
2007	16	17	48%	4.9	4.8
2008	16	17	48%	4.6	4.4
2009	20	14	59%	5.6	4.5
TOTAL	110	94	54%	4.9	4.7

BILL MILLER

Full name William Scott Miller
Born May 31, 1967, Vallejo, California
Umpired First Game: July 28, 1997
Height: 6' 2" Weight: 215
Ejections: 1997 (1), 2000 (4), 2001 (4), 2002 (1), 2003 (3), 2005 (4), 2006 (4),
2007 (5), 2008 (2). Total: 28

Miller has been a consistent pitcher's umpire since he joined the major league staff in 1999, for good reason. He'll usually give pitchers the high strike, low strike, and allow them to stretch the corners a little as well. The strike zone stays the same, however. Miller is a pretty solid under umpire.

Year	Over	Under	%	Runs/Gm	Strike
2004	15	18	45%	9	63.8%
2005	13	18	42%	8.1	63.6%
2006	16	17	48%	10.2	63.8%
2007	15	19	44%	9.8	63.2%
2008	12	21	36%	7.9	63.6%
2009	10	23	30%	8.9	63.6%
TOTAL	81	116	41%	9	63.6%

Year	H Win	H Lose	Win%	Home R/G	Road R/G
2004	16	18	47%	4.3	4.7
2005	20	13	61%	4.3	3.8
2006	15	19	44%	5.2	5.0
2007	13	21	38%	4.7	5.1
2008	23	13	64%	4.0	3.9
2009	16	19	46%	4.5	4.5
TOTAL	103	103	50%	4.5	4.5

ED MONTAGUE

Full name Edward Michael Montague
Born November 3, 1948, San Francisco, California
Umpired First Game: October 1, 1974
Height: 5' 11" Weight: 170
Son of Ed Montague
Ejections: 1976 (3), 1977 (8), 1979 (1), 1980 (2), 1981 (2), 1982 (3), 1983 (2),
1986 (1), 1987 (1), 1988 (1), 1989 (1), 1990 (2), 1992 (1), 1994 (1), 1995 (1), 1996
(1), 1997 (2), 1998 (2), 1999 (1), 2000 (5), 2001 (4), 2002 (1), 2003 (1), 2004 (1),
2005 (1), 2006 (2), 2007 (3), 2008 (1). Total: 55

Montegue is yet another umpire that grew up in the inner circle of baseball. His
father, Ed Sr., played baseball for the Indians and was later a longtime scout for
the Giants where he signed Willie Mays away from the Negro League
Birmingham Black Bears. Montegue has been a major league umpire since 1976.
He is extremely consistent and one of the best in the game behind the plate.

Year	Over	Under	%	Runs/Gm	Strike
2004	15	14	52%	10.3	62.2%
2005	21	8	72%	11	63.0%
2006	15	6	71%	11.2	61.8%
2007	16	14	53%	10.2	61.8%
2008	8	16	33%	7.8	61.7%
2009	4	1	80%	11.8	61.3%
TOTAL	79	59	57%	10.4	62.0%

Year	H Win	H Lose	Win%	Home R/G	Road R/G
2004	15	16	48.4	5.5	4.8
2005	14	19	42.4	5.1	5.9
2006	15	7	68.2	6.6	4.6
2007	18	13	58.1	5.3	4.9
2008	15	10	60	4.4	3.4
2009	2	3	40	5.8	6.0
TOTAL	79	68	53%	5.4	4.7

PAUL NAUERT

Full name Paul Edward Nauert
Born July 7, 1963, Louisville, Kentucky
Umpired First Game: May 19, 1995
Height: 6' 1" Weight: 200
Ejections: 1998 (3), 1999 (3), 2004 (3), 2005 (1), 2006 (1), 2007 (3), 2008 (1).
Total: 15

Nauert spent five years in the International League before being offered a major league job in 1999. One of nine children in his family, Nauert lost his job during the umpire strike in 1999 but regained it in 2002 when an arbitrator ruled MLB had wrongly terminated his contract. He has a large strike zone that leans under.

Year	Over	Under	%	Runs/Gm	Strike
2004	15	18	45%	8.6	63.2%
2005	16	18	47%	8.8	63.8%
2006	17	16	52%	9.2	62.6%
2007	19	13	59%	10.3	63.1%
2008	15	18	45%	9.1	63.2%
2009	17	16	52%	9.6	63.3%
TOTAL	99	99	50%	9.3	63.2%

Year	H Win	H Lose	Win%	Home R/G	Road R/G
2004	17	17	50%	4.1	4.5
2005	16	18	47%	3.9	4.9
2006	18	16	53%	4.8	4.4
2007	19	16	54%	5.1	5.2
2008	13	20	39%	4.2	4.9
2009	13	21	38%	5.4	4.1
	96	108	47%	4.6	4.7

JEFF NELSON

Full name Jeffrey Brian Nelson
Born June 1, 1965, St. Paul, Minnesota
Umpired First Game: May 9, 1997
Height: 6' 2" Weight: 196
Ejections: 1998 (3), 1999 (1), 2000 (3), 2001 (3), 2002 (3), 2003 (1), 2004 (2),
2005 (5), 2006 (1), 2007 (1), 2008 (4).
Total: 27

Nelson began umpiring professionally after attending the Joe Brinkman Umpire School where he was chosen the top prospect in 1989. He earned a major league job in 1999, and was behind the plate when Mark McGwire hit his 500th career home run. Nelson got his bit of notoriety in the playoffs when he mistakenly gave Jermaine Dye first base on what was a foul ball rather than a hit batsman. The next batter hit a grand slam. He missed a chunk of 2007 to undergo treatment for cancer. As of now, his cancer is in remission. Nelson had been a solid under umpire until the 2009 season.

Year	Over	Under	%	Runs/Gm	Strike
2004	13	17	43%	9	62.3%
2005	14	15	48%	8.8	63.2%
2006	12	20	38%	9.2	62.8%
2007	4	15	21%	5.9	63.1%
2008	14	18	44%	8.5	63.7%
2009	22	11	67%	10.6	62.3%
TOTAL	79	96	45%	8.7	62.9%

Year	H Win	H Lose	Win%	Home R/G	Road R/G
2004	15	16	48%	4.3	4.7
2005	15	18	45%	4.0	4.8
2006	22	11	67%	5.1	4.1
2007	12	8	60%	2.9	3.0
2008	21	12	64%	4.5	4.0
2009	18	16	53%	5.4	5.2
	103	81	56%	4.3	4.3

BRIAN O'NORA

Full name Brian Keith O'Nora
Born February 7, 1963, Youngstown, Ohio
Umpired First Game: August 4, 1992
Height: 6' 1" Weight: 210
Ejections: 1994 (1), 1995 (1), 1996 (4), 1998 (2), 1999 (6), 2000 (2), 2001 (1),
2003 (3), 2005 (1), 2006 (2), 2007 (1), 2008 (1), 2009 (2). Total: 27

A rather inconsistent umpire, O'Nora has been a full-time major league umpire since 1999. He has a very big strike zone which tends to make his games go under.

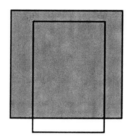

Year	Over	Under	%	Runs/Gm	Strike
2004	11	18	38%	8.3	62.0%
2005	14	19	42%	9.1	63.5%
2006	19	12	61%	10.6	63.1%
2007	10	6	63%	10.3	62.4%
2008	12	20	38%	8.6	63.5%
2009	16	18	47%	8.5	63.1%
TOTAL	**82**	**93**	**47%**	**9.2**	**62.9%**

Year	H Win	H Lose	Win%	Home R/G	Road R/G
2004	12	17	41%	3.7	4.6
2005	18	17	51%	4.3	4.8
2006	17	16	52%	5.1	5.6
2007	9	9	50%	4.3	6.1
2008	19	15	56%	4.2	4.4
2009	17	17	50%	4.6	4.0
TOTAL	**92**	**91**	**50%**	**4.4**	**4.9**

ED RAPUANO

Full name Edward Stephen Jr. Rapuano
Born September 30, 1957, New Haven, Connecticut
Umpired First Game: May 11, 1990
Height: 5' 10" Weight: 190
Ejections: 1991 (4), 1992 (5), 1993 (3), 1995 (4), 1996 (3), 1997 (4), 2000 (1),
2001 (2), 2002 (2), 2003 (3), 2004 (3), 2006 (2), 2007 (3), 2008 (4), 2009 (4).
Total: 47

A major league umpire since 1991, Rapuano is one of the better umpires in the game today. His strike zone is small, but he shows good judgment everywhere else and maintains control of the game. His hobbies include playing golf and winemaking. He has umpired in the World Series in 2001 and 2003, as well as the All-Star game in 1995. He has also worked in five League Championship Series (1999, 2000, 2002, 2004, 2005) and five Division Series (1997, 1998, 2001, 2003, 2006), and the NL's one-game wild card playoff in 1999.

Year	Over	Under	%	Runs/Gm	Strike
2004	17	15	53%	9.6	62.4%
2005	16	18	47%	8.9	62.5%
2006	14	20	41%	9.5	62.0%
2007	12	21	36%	8.5	62.1%
2008	17	14	55%	9.7	62.2%
2009	16	17	48%	8.9	62.0%
TOTAL	**92**	**105**	**47%**	**9.2**	**62.2%**

Year	H Win	H Lose	Win%	Home R/G	Road R/G
2004	18	16	53%	4.7	4.9
2005	14	21	40%	4.1	4.8
2006	16	18	47%	4.2	5.3
2007	22	12	65%	4.4	4.1
2008	15	19	44%	4.7	4.9
2009	21	14	60%	4.8	4.4
TOTAL	**106**	**100**	**51%**	**4.8**	**4.4**

RICK REED

Full name Rick Alan Reed
Born March 3, 1950, Detroit, Michigan
Umpired First Game: May 9, 1979
Height: 6' 0" Weight: 207
Ejections: 1979 (1), 1980 (1), 1981 (1), 1982 (1), 1983 (4), 1984 (2), 1985 (1),
1986 (1), 1987 (1), 1989 (1), 1990 (2), 1991 (5), 1992 (3), 1994 (6), 1995 (3), 1996
(2), 1998 (2), 1999 (2), 2000 (3), 2001 (5), 2002 (2), 2004 (1), 2005 (1), 2006 (8),
2008 (1), 2009 (1). Total: 62

A part-time actor in the off-season, Reed was the home plate umpire in Kevin Costner's move "For the Love of the Game", one of the worst baseball movies ever made. He has been around the block a few times. Reed became a full time major league umpire in 1983. He is a solid umpire, with a large but consistent strike zone. He has worked in 7 postseasons, including the 1991 World Series; the American League Championship Series in 1989, 1995, and 1999; and the Division Series in 1997, 2000, and 2001. He worked the All-Star Game in 1986 and 1998.

Year	Over	Under	%	Runs/Gm	Strike
2004	13	12	52%	8.8	60.5%
2005	13	14	48%	8.5	63.1%
2006	16	16	50%	9.3	62.3%
2007	16	14	53%	9.7	62.7%
2008	7	6	54%	8.5	61.2%
2009	4	7	36%	9.1	62.4%
TOTAL	69	69	50%	9	62.0%

Year	H Win	H Lose	Win%	Home R/G	Road R/G
2004	15	11	58%	4.3	4.5
2005	15	15	50%	3.8	4.7
2006	18	14	56%	4.7	4.6
2007	21	12	64%	4.9	4.8
2008	5	8	38%	3.9	4.5
2009	7	4	64%	5.3	3.8
TOTAL	81	64	56%	4.2	4.7

MIKE REILLY

Full name Michael Eugene Reilly
Born July 2, 1949, Sioux City, Iowa
Umpired First Game: April 11, 1977
Height: 6' 0" Weight: 180
Ejections: 1977 (2), 1978 (5), 1979 (2), 1980 (1), 1981 (2), 1982 (8), 1983 (4),
1984 (3), 1985 (3), 1986 (1), 1987 (3), 1988 (3), 1990 (1), 1991 (1), 1992 (1), 1993
(2), 1995 (1), 1996 (1), 1997 (1), 1998 (6), 2000 (2), 2004 (2), 2005 (1), 2006 (1),
2007 (1), 2008 (1), 2009 (1). Total: 60

Reilly is a long time MLB umpire who is considered one of the best umps in the game today. He began his career in the majors in 1977, and has a small but consistent strike zone. Reilly grew up in Iowa, but currently lives in Battle Creek Michigan with his wife and four children. On the board of directors for Big Brothers/Big Sisters, Reilly also does a lot of charity work with the Food Bank in Michigan. One of the few umpires with a printable nickname, Reilly was called "Corn Flakes" by Ernie Harwell because of his Battle Creek hometown.

Year	Over	Under	%	Runs/Gm	Strike
2004	19	14	58%	10.8	62.0%
2005	13	14	48%	9.8	62.3%
2006	14	18	44%	8.9	63.5%
2007	17	15	53%	10.1	61.9%
2008	19	15	56%	9.4	62.6%
2009	19	14	58%	9.7	62.0%
TOTAL	101	90	53%	9.8	62.4%

Year	H Win	H Lose	Win%	Home R/G	Road R/G
2004	16	18	47%	5.0	5.8
2005	20	8	71%	5.7	4.1
2006	19	15	56%	4.9	3.9
2007	17	17	50%	4.9	5.3
2008	18	16	53%	5.0	4.5
2009	15	19	44%	4.5	5.2
TOTAL	105	93	53%	5.1	4.7

CHARLIE RELIFORD

Full name Charles Harold Reliford
Born September 19, 1956, Ashland, Kentucky
Umpired First Game: May 29, 1989
Height: 5' 9" Weight: 190
Ejections: 1990 (1), 1991 (3), 1992 (4), 1993 (5), 1994 (3), 1995 (3), 1996 (3),
1997 (3), 1998 (2), 1999 (2), 2000 (2), 2001 (4), 2002 (2), 2003 (2), 2004 (4), 2005
(2), 2006 (6), 2007 (1), 2008 (2). Total: 54

Reliford was a catcher before trading in his glove for an umpire's mask. He joined the major league staff in 1991 and is now the chief instructor for the Wendelstedt Umpire School. He is a solid umpire with a small strike zone. His games lean to the over. He umpired in the World Series in 2000 and 2004, and in the All-Star Game in 1996. He has also worked in three League Championship Series (1999, 2001, and 2002) and in four Division Series (1995, 1997, 2000, and 2004).

Year	Over	Under	%	Runs/Gm	Strike
2004	11	18	38%	7.9	61.5%
2005	8	5	62%	11.4	63.7%
2006	13	10	57%	9.6	63.8%
2007	14	11	56%	9.5	63.1%
2008	14	13	52%	10.1	62.3%
2009	7	13	35%	7.8	63.8%
TOTAL	67	70	49%	9.4	63.0%

Year	H Win	H Lose	Win%	Home R/G	Road R/G
2004	16	14	53%	3.9	4.0
2005	7	7	50%	5.6	5.7
2006	11	14	44%	4.6	5.1
2007	14	11	56%	4.8	4.7
2008	17	11	61%	5.9	4.3
2009	9	13	41%	3.9	4.0
TOTAL	74	70	51%	4.8	4.6

JIM REYNOLDS

Full name James Norris Reynolds
Born December 22, 1968, Marlborough, Massachusetts
Umpired First Game: June 4, 1999
Height: 5' 11" Weight: 185
Ejections: 1999 (1), 2000 (2), 2001 (4), 2002 (1), 2003 (3), 2004 (7), 2005 (1),
2006 (2), 2007 (2), 2008 (1). Total: 24

Reynolds has been a major league umpire since 1999. He began umpiring after earning a degree in journalism from Connecticut in 1991. He is a solid umpire with large strike zone, but for some reason his games tend to go over. He won't call the low strike at times. Reynolds's post-season experience includes the 2004 All-Star game and the 2005 American League Division Series playoffs between the Yankees and Anaheim.

Year	Over	Under	%	Runs/Gm	Strike
2004	16	14	53%	9.2	63.3%
2005	16	17	48%	9.1	62.4%
2006	15	15	50%	9.2	62.0%
2007	20	13	61%	10.4	62.7%
2008	21	11	66%	10.3	62.7%
2009	18	11	62%	9.7	62.8%
TOTAL	**106**	**81**	**57%**	**9.7**	**62.7%**

Year	H Win	H Lose	Win%	Home R/G	Road R/G
2004	21	12	64%	4.4	4.8
2005	15	20	43%	4.3	4.8
2006	17	16	52%	4.6	4.7
2007	20	15	57%	5.1	5.3
2008	16	19	46%	5.0	5.3
2009	19	10	66%	5.2	4.7
TOTAL	**108**	**92**	**54%**		

BRIAN RUNGE

Full name Brian Edward Runge
Born January 5, 1970, San Diego, California
Umpired First Game: April 23, 1999
Height: 6' 1" Weight: 225
Son of Paul Runge
Grandson of Ed Runge
Ejections: 2000 (1), 2001 (1), 2006 (1), 2007 (1), 2008 (3), 2009 (1).
Total: 8

Runge is a legacy umpire. His father, Paul, was a long time National League umpire and his grandfather, Ed, umpired for 26 years in the American League. The Runge family is the first three-generation umpire family in Major League baseball. Runge grew up a Padre fan, and his grandfather Ed worked in the Padre community relations department until his death three years ago. Brian Runge still lives in San Diego with his wife and two children. He is an under umpire.

Year	Over	Under	%	Runs/Gm	Strike
2004	10	20	33%	8	63.5%
2005	2	5	29%	5.8	64.4%
2006	15	14	52%	9.7	63.4%
2007	18	15	55%	9.9	62.9%
2008	14	17	45%	9.1	63.6%
2009	6	16	27%	7.9	63.3%
TOTAL	65	87	43%	8.4	63.5%

Year	H Win	H Lose	Win%	Home R/G	Road R/G
2004	20	11	65%	4.2	3.8
2005	6	2	75%	3.1	2.6
2006	15	18	45%	4.6	5.1
2007	17	19	47%	4.7	5.2
2008	18	16	53%	4.4	4.8
2009	17	7	71%	4.7	4.3
TOTAL	93	73	56%		

PAUL SCHRIEBER

Full name Paul Warren Schrieber
Born June 30, 1966, Eugene, Oregon
Umpired First Game: June 6, 1997
Height: 5' 11" Weight: 190
Ejections: 1998 (1), 2000 (1), 2001 (2), 2004 (1), 2005 (3), 2006 (5), 2007 (2), 2008 (4), 2009 (2)
Total: 21

Schrieber joined the MLB staff in 1998 after spending eight years in the minors. He is a decent umpire overall, but is rather weak in the consistency of his ball/strikes calls. He seems to have a small, moving strike zone. Up until 2005, Schrieber's games tended to go over. A graduate of Portland State University, Schrieber's father was an umpire who made it as far as AAA before hanging it up.

Year	Over	Under	%	Runs/Gm	Strike
2004	25	8	76%	12.1	61.2%
2005	11	15	42%	8.4	61.9%
2006	14	13	52%	9.2	61.6%
2007	17	14	55%	9.8	60.9%
2008	15	15	50%	9.7	60.3%
2009	14	16	47%	9.6	61.5%
TOTAL	**96**	**81**	**54%**	**9.8**	**61.2%**

Year	H Win	H Lose	Win%	Home R/G	Road R/G
2004	17	17	50%	6.0	6.1
2005	10	17	37%	3.7	4.7
2006	15	14	52%	4.8	4.5
2007	14	17	45%	4.4	5.4
2008	17	13	57%	4.9	4.7
2009	16	17	48%	4.8	4.8
TOTAL	**89**	**95**	**48%**		

DALE SCOTT

Full name Dale Allan Scott
Born August 14, 1959, Eugene, Oregon
Umpired First Game: August 19, 1985
Height: 6' 0" Weight: 190
Ejections: 1986 (5), 1987 (5), 1988 (3), 1989 (1), 1990 (1), 1991 (3), 1992 (1),
1993 (14), 1994 (2), 1995 (3), 1996 (1), 1997 (1), 1998 (4), 1999 (2), 2000 (3),
2001 (5), 2003 (1), 2004 (1), 2005 (6), 2006 (5), 2007 (1), 2008 (2).
Total: 70

A native of Oregon, Scott has an A.S in television broadcasting and would have been a disc jockey had he not become an umpire. Scott has been in the majors since 1986, just 4 years after graduating from Umpiring School. He is a very good umpire, maintaining control of the game and with a consistent strike zone. He has worked the World Series in 1998, 2001 and 2004, and in the All-Star Game in 1993 and 2001. Scott has also umpired in four League Championship Series (1996, 1999, 2000, and 2002) and in seven Division Series (1995, 1997, 1998, 2001, 2003, 2004, and 2005.

Year	Over	Under	%	Runs/Gm	Strike
2004	13	17	43%	8.8	62.9%
2005	16	17	48%	9.4	62.4%
2006	16	15	52%	9.6	62.5%
2007	16	16	50%	9.6	62.9%
2008	12	20	38%	9.4	62.1%
2009	18	16	53%	8.9	62.8%
TOTAL	**91**	**101**	**47%**	**9.3**	**62.6%**

Year	H Win	H Lose	Win%	Home R/G	Road R/G
2004	14	18	44%	4.4	4.4
2005	20	14	59%	5.4	4.0
2006	16	19	46%	4.4	5.2
2007	19	16	54%	4.6	5.0
2008	21	13	62%	5.2	4.2
2009	19	15	56%	4.7	4.2
TOTAL	**109**	**95**	**53%**		

TIM TIMMONS

Full name Timothy Forbes Timmons
Born December 30, 1967, Columbus, Ohio
Umpired First Game: September 3, 1999
Height: 6' 0" Weight: 190
Ejections: 2000 (4), 2001 (6), 2002 (5), 2003 (4), 2004 (5), 2005 (4), 2006 (5),
2007 (4), 2008 (7).
Total: 44

Timmons became a major league umpire in 2001 after spending 10 years in the minor leagues. A graduate of Ohio State University, Timmons spends off-seasons in Columbus, Ohio selling real estate with his wife. Their business motto is brilliant: "Team Timmons: You're Safe At Home". They have three children, not counting the Porsches that Timmons refurbishes in his spare time. His strike zone tends to be inconsistent from game to game.

Year	Over	Under	%	Runs/Gm	Strike
2004	8	21	28%	7.5	62.4%
2005	18	15	55%	9.9	62.9%
2006	14	19	42%	9.5	62.6%
2007	14	19	42%	9.1	61.8%
2008	18	15	55%	10.1	62.6%
2009	19	13	59%	10.7	62.9%
TOTAL	112	90	56%	9.9	62.7%

Year	H Win	H Lose	Win%	Home R/G	Road R/G
2004	16	15	52%	3.7	3.9
2005	23	12	66%	5.1	4.8
2006	19	16	54%	4.9	4.7
2007	23	10	70%	5.0	4.0
2008	15	19	44%	4.9	5.2
2009	16	18	47%	4.6	6.1
TOTAL	91	102	47%		

TIM TSCHIDA

Full name Timothy Joseph Tschida
Born May 4, 1960, St. Paul, Minnesota
Umpired First Game: July 24, 1985
Height: 5' 9" Weight: 180
Ejections: 1986 (2), 1987 (3), 1988 (4), 1989 (1), 1990 (3), 1991 (3), 1992 (2),
1993 (2), 1994 (4), 1995 (3), 1996 (4), 1997 (2), 1998 (14), 1999 (2), 2000 (4),
2001 (3), 2002 (4), 2003 (3), 2004 (3), 2005 (1), 2006 (5), 2007 (2), 2008 (2), 2009
(3). Total: 79

Tschida's claim to fame outside umpiring is meeting the last five American Presidents. An umpire since 1986, he is a solid umpire with a large strike zone. He has worked in seven postseasons, including the World Series in 1998 and 2002; the League Championship Series in 1993, 1999, 2000, and 2001; and the Division Series in 1996, 1997, 1998, 2001, 2002, and 2006. He was also the third base umpire for Kenny Rogers' perfect game on July 28, 1994. He was an

Year	Over	Under	%	Runs/Gm	Strike
2004	15	18	45%	9.2	62.8%
2005	14	19	42%	9.2	62.7%
2006	15	19	44%	9.3	63.5%
2007	17	17	50%	9.7	62.5%
2008	20	13	61%	9.9	62.3%
2009	18	12	60%	11.3	61.5%
TOTAL	110	93	54%	9.6	62.5%

Year	H Win	H Lose	Win%	Home R/G	Road R/G
2004	18	16	53%	4.4	4.8
2005	20	13	61%	4.9	4.3
2006	16	19	46%	4.5	4.9
2007	20	15	57%	5.4	4.3
2008	21	13	62%	5.1	4.8
2009	15	17	47%	6.0	5.4
TOTAL	99	98	50%		

LARRY VANOVER

Full name Larry Wayne Vanover
Born August 22, 1955, Owensboro, Kentucky
Umpired First Game: June 25, 1991
Height: 5' 11" Weight: 210
Ejections: 1993 (3), 1994 (7), 1995 (4), 1996 (1), 1997 (6), 1998 (1), 1999 (1),
2002 (3), 2003 (2), 2004 (3), 2005 (3), 2006 (1), 2007 (5), 2008 (3), 2009 (5).
Total: 48

Vanover started umpiring as a hobby and turned it into a career after graduating from the University of Kentucky with a degree in Architecture. He earned a major league spot in 1993, but lost it when he resigned/was fired during the Richie Phillips-led umpire strike in 1999. After an arbitrator ruled MLB had wrongly fired him, Vanover was back behind the plate in 2002. He isn't a very good umpire; his work calling strikes is inconsistent and uneven. He doesn't give the low strike to pitchers.

Year	Over	Under	%	Runs/Gm	Strike
2004	16	17	48%	9.7	61.5%
2005	11	20	35%	8.2	63.4%
2006	20	14	59%	9.7	63.2%
2007	23	13	64%	11.2	62.4%
2008	17	12	59%	10.1	61.7%
2009	15	18	45%	8.5	62.3%
TOTAL	102	94	52%	9.6	62.4%

Year	H Win	H Lose	Win%	Home R/G	Road R/G
2004	20	15	57%	5.2	4.5
2005	16	18	47%	3.8	4.5
2006	20	15	57%	5.2	4.5
2007	25	11	69%	6.4	4.8
2008	14	18	44%	4.4	5.7
2009	22	12	65%	3.4	4.9
TOTAL	117	89	57%	4.7	4.8

MARK WEGNER

Full name Mark Patrick Wegner
Born March 4, 1972, St. Paul, Minnesota
Umpired First Game: May 20, 1998
Height: 5' 8" Weight: 180
Ejections: 1998 (1), 2000 (3), 2001 (4), 2002 (3), 2003 (11), 2004 (4), 2005 (1), 2006 (5), 2007 (6), 2008 (5), 2009 (4).
Total: 47

Wegner is the shortest umpire in baseball, but still has difficulty calling the low strike. He makes up for it with the rest of the strike zone however. His games have trended under the last couple of seasons.

Year	Over	Under	%	Runs/Gm	Strike
2004	16	11	59%	10.2	61.5%
2005	13	20	39%	8.7	62.8%
2006	19	13	59%	9.1	61.7%
2007	17	13	57%	9.5	62.2%
2008	15	18	45%	9.3	61.7%
2009	17	19	47%	8.9	62.5%
TOTAL	**97**	**94**	**51%**	**9.3**	**62.1%**

Year	H Win	H Lose	Win%	Home R/G	Road R/G
2004	15	15	50%	4.4	5.7
2005	17	17	50%	4.2	4.5
2006	21	12	64%	5.0	4.2
2007	14	19	42%	4.4	5.1
2008	22	13	63%	5.3	4.1
2009	21	14	60%	4.2	4.8
TOTAL	**110**	**90**	**55%**	**4.6**	**4.7**

BILL WELKE

Full name William Anthony Welke
Born August 22, 1967, Coldwater, Michigan
Umpired First Game: June 4, 1999
Height: 6' 2" Weight: 240
Brother of Tim Welke
Ejections: 1999 (1), 2000 (8), 2001 (9), 2002 (4), 2003 (6), 2004 (3), 2005 (6), 2006 (3), 2007 (6), 2008 (4). Total: 50

Welke, married with four children, grew up in Coldwater Michigan and lives currently in Marshall Michigan. He joined the major league staff in 1999 after umpiring in the minors for 8 years. In the past Welke was generally a neutral umpire but that has shifted towards the over the last couple of years. He seems to call the strike zone the way umpires should.

Year	Over	Under	%	Runs/Gm	Strike
2004	11	21	34%	8.5	64.0%
2005	18	16	53%	9.1	63.8%
2006	14	18	44%	9	63.7%
2007	17	17	50%	9.1	63.4%
2008	19	14	58%	10.3	62.6%
2009	17	12	59%	10.7	62.7%
TOTAL	96	98	49%	9.5	63.4%

Year	H Win	H Lose	Win%	Home R/G	Road R/G
2004	18	15	55%	3.9	4.6
2005	16	19	46%	4.9	4.2
2006	17	17	50%	4.6	4.4
2007	17	18	49%	4.4	4.7
2008	25	9	74%	6.3	4.0
2009	18	15	55%	5.7	5.0
TOTAL	111	93	54%		

TIM WELKE

Full name Timothy James Welke
Born August 23, 1957, Pontiac, Michigan
Umpired First Game: June 14, 1983
Height: 6' 3" Weight: 230
Brother of Bill Welke
Ejections: 1983 (3), 1984 (2), 1985 (3), 1986 (5), 1987 (5), 1988 (7), 1989 (1),
1990 (2), 1991 (7), 1992 (3), 1993 (1), 1994 (1), 1995 (1), 1996 (7), 1998 (4), 1999
(4), 2000 (1), 2001 (1), 2002 (3), 2003 (1), 2004 (2), 2005 (1), 2006 (1), 2007 (1).
Total: 67

Welke is one of the better umpires in the game, particularly behind the plate. A veteran umpire who first joined the major league staff in 1984, Welke had the privilege of making the cover of Sports Illustrated in 1998 with the heading "KILL THE UMPS". Heavily involved in Big Brothers/Big Sisters in Michigan, Welke's younger brother Bill is also a major league umpire.

Year	Over	Under	%	Runs/Gm	Strike
2004	13	18	42%	8.2	62.6%
2005	12	19	39%	9.3	63.1%
2006	15	18	45%	10.6	63.1%
2007	13	10	57%	10	63.3%
2008	17	15	53%	9.4	63.5%
2009	16	11	59%	11.3	62.1%
TOTAL	86	91	49%	9.8	63.0%

Year	H Win	H Lose	Win%	Home R/G	Road R/G
2004	22	10	69%	4.9	3.3
2005	17	17	50%	4.4	4.9
2006	20	15	57%	5.2	5.4
2007	12	12	50%	5.6	4.4
2008	15	19	44%	4.3	5.1
2009	14	14	50%	5.6	5.6
TOTAL	100	87	53%		

HUNTER WENDELSTEDT

Full name Harry Hunter III Wendelstedt
Born June 22, 1971, Atlanta, Georgia
Umpired First Game: April 19, 1998
Height: 6' 1" Weight: 220
Son of Harry Wendelstedt
Ejections: 1998 (3), 1999 (3), 2000 (3), 2001 (6), 2002 (2), 2003 (2), 2004 (5),
2005 (4), 2006 (6), 2007 (4), 2008 (4), 2009 (5).
Total: 47

The son of long time National League Umpire Harvey Wendelstedt, Hunter has been working in the majors since 1999. Overall Wendelstedt is a solid umpire but at times is too confrontational with players and managers. He had a nasty run-in with Ozzie Guillen in 2004; Guillen was initially suspended for two games for excessive arguing, then received an additional two game suspension when Guillen claimed Wendelstedt lied on the umpire report following the game.

Year	Over	Under	%	Runs/Gm	Strike
2004	23	10	70%	10.8	60.6%
2005	13	17	43%	9.1	64.1%
2006	18	14	56%	10.2	63.1%
2007	14	19	42%	8.6	62.3%
2008	19	13	59%	9.8	62.7%
2009	16	19	46%	9.1	61.9%
TOTAL	**103**	**92**	**53%**	**9.6**	**62.5%**

Year	H Win	H Lose	Win%	Home R/G	Road R/G
2004	17	16	52%	5.1	5.7
2005	21	11	66%	4.7	4.4
2006	16	17	48%	4.9	5.4
2007	17	16	52%	4.2	4.4
2008	21	14	60%	5.2	4.7
2009	16	19	46%	4.2	4.8
TOTAL	**108**	**93**	**54%**		

JOE WEST

Full name Joseph Henry West
Born October 31, 1952, Asheville, North Carolina
Umpired First Game: September 14, 1976
Height: 6' 1" Weight: 275
Ejections: 1977 (2), 1978 (6), 1980 (3), 1981 (2), 1982 (2), 1983 (4), 1985 (6),
1986 (2), 1987 (7), 1988 (6), 1989 (5), 1990 (5), 1991 (5), 1992 (4), 1993 (3), 1994
(6), 1996 (4), 1997 (3), 1998 (7), 1999 (1), 2002 (4), 2003 (11), 2004 (3), 2006 (10),
2007 (7), 2008 (6), 2009 (6). Total: 130

Cowboy Joe joined the major league staff in 1978, and has created waves ever since. West was an outstanding quarterback for Elon College before starting to umpire soon after graduation. He is an accomplished singer/songwriter. West has performed with Merle Haggard, Mickey Gilley, Box Car Willie, TG Shepard and scores of others at the Grand Ole Opry. A real renaissance man, West is also a terrible umpire. Not a bad musician though; if you want his CD titled "Blue Cowboy" it is available at www.cowboyjoewest.com. It is only $10.95 and has 11 outstanding songs, including a sharp country version of "Take Me Out To the Ballgame".

Year	Over	Under	%	Runs/Gm	Strike
2004	21	14	60%	10.1	62.3%
2005	16	18	47%	9.4	63.7%
2006	17	17	50%	10.3	61.9%
2007	18	17	51%	9.1	62.1%
2008	16	13	55%	10.2	62.7%
2009	16	18	47%	9.3	61.5%
TOTAL	104	97	52%	9.7	62.4%

Year	H Win	H Lose	Win%	Home R/G	Road R/G
2004	26	10	72%	6.0	4.1
2005	16	19	46%	4.3	5.1
2006	15	19	44%	4.8	5.5
2007	18	19	49%	4.7	4.4
2008	14	19	42%	5.1	5.1
2009	20	14	59%	5.2	4.2
TOTAL	109	100	52%		

MIKE WINTERS

Full name Michael John Winters
Born November 19, 1958, Carlsbad, California
Umpired First Game: July 9, 1988
Height: 6' 1" Weight: 195
Ejections: 1989 (1), 1990 (3), 1991 (5), 1992 (2), 1993 (4), 1994 (4), 1995 (4),
1996 (4), 1997 (5), 1998 (6), 1999 (7), 2000 (6), 2001 (5), 2002 (4), 2003 (4), 2004
(3), 2005 (1), 2006 (1), 2007 (7), 2008 (5). Total: 81

Winters has been a major league umpire since 1990. A graduate of San Diego State University, Winters has umpired both Tony Gwynn's and Cal Ripken's 3000th hit as well as Mark McGwire's 62nd home run in 1998. He has worked the 1995 All-Star Game, six Division Series (1998, 1999, 2000, 2001, 2002, and 2006), the 1997 and 2004 National League Championship Series and the 2002 and 2006 World Series. An altercation with Milton Bradley in September 2007 resulted in a suspension for Winters; he has a reputation as being prickly sort around baseball.

Year	Over	Under	%	Runs/Gm	Strike
2004	18	14	56%	10	62.6%
2005	13	21	38%	8.9	62.0%
2006	14	16	47%	9.4	63.0%
2007	16	15	52%	9.3	63.0%
2008	14	16	47%	8.9	62.1%
2009	15	16	48%	8.9	62.9%
TOTAL	**90**	**98**	**48%**	**9.2**	**62.6%**

Year	H Win	H Lose	Win%	Home R/G	Road R/G
2004	18	16	53%	4.8	5.2
2005	23	12	66%	4.9	3.9
2006	16	16	50%	4.5	4.9
2007	16	16	50%	4.3	5.1
2008	19	12	61%	5.1	3.8
2009	21	10	68%	5.2	3.7
TOTAL	**113**	**82**	**58%**		

JIM WOLF

Full name James Michael Wolf
Born July 24, 1969, West Hills, California
Umpired First Game: September 2, 1999
Height: 6' 0" Weight: 195
Brother of Randy Wolf
Ejections: 2001 (2), 2002 (1), 2003 (1), 2004 (3), 2005 (4), 2006 (1), 2007 (1),
2008 (1), 2009 (3).
Total: 17

Wolf was given a full-time spot on the major league staff when Mark Hirschbeck decided to retire following an injury during the 2004 season. The older brother of Dodgers pitcher Randy Wolf, Jim was a catcher in college before choosing to umpire in the minor leagues. He is not permitted by MLB to work home plate when his brother is on the mound, but can work the bases. This has caused some whispers around the league, but for the most part it is dismissed by managers of the opposing teams.

Year	Over	Under	%	Runs/Gm	Strike
2004	15	16	48%	9.6	62.1%
2005	16	17	48%	9	63.7%
2006	19	12	61%	10.6	62.9%
2007	12	20	38%	8.8	63.8%
2008	16	17	48%	9.3	62.5%
2009	18	14	56%	9.9	62.1%
TOTAL	96	96	50%	9.5	62.9%

Year	H Win	H Lose	Win%	Home R/G	Road R/G
2004	21	12	64%	5.7	4.0
2005	17	18	49%	4.5	4.6
2006	18	14	56%	5.4	5.1
2007	20	13	61%	4.6	4.3
2008	17	18	49%	4.0	5.3
2009	20	13	61%	5.7	4.2
TOTAL	113	88	56%		

Breinigsville, PA USA
07 March 2010
233651BV00002B/1/P

9 780977 878703